EXERCISING YOUR SOUL

EXERCISING YOUR SOUL

+ + +

FIFTEEN MINUTES
A DAY TO A SPIRITUAL LIFE

GARY JANSEN

New York   Boston   Nashville

FaithWords
Hachette Book Group
237 Park Avenue
New York, NY 10017

Printed in the United States of America

FaithWords is a division of Hachette Book Group, Inc.
The FaithWords name and logo are trademarks of Hachette Book Group, Inc.

ISBN-13: 978-0-446-53953-1

For my wife, Grace,
and my sons Eddie and Charlie,
the joys of my life.

CONTENTS

Pray constantly.
Saint Paul

AUTHOR'S NOTE

This little book you have in your hands is essentially a book on prayer. Not the namby-pamby, rattling-off-a-wish-list, "Oh, please let me have nice things" kind of prayer. (Who am I kidding?—just five minutes ago I asked to win the lottery.) I'm talking about prayer that will, by divine grace, help you experience God boldly, deeply, and intimately. This collection of reflections, anecdotes, stories, and exercises may appear to be masquerading as a self-help book. I can assure you it is no such thing. *Exercising Your Soul* is a *God-help* book, not because I have delusions of being the Creator of the universe, but because all life, all people, all things—all assistance—come from God. If this book helps you in any way, it is not my doing but because God desires every one of us to know him more fully.

Much talk is made of the idea of grace, God's unmerited gift of love to us, as if the Lord created some people to receive this blessing and others not. For all I know, this may be true—maybe God does play favorites—but I don't believe this. God is ever-present in all of creation. You. Me. That annoying person at your job. That waffle you ate this morning. The coffee cup you just threw away. *Everything.*

Many of us may already believe this, but the trick is not perceiving these words in the mind, but *feeling* them in the heart. It is only when the words are made flesh by sensory experience, by the incarnating of them by the Holy Spirit, that life truly begins. This is when we experience grace. This is when we experience Christ.

Grace, in some ways, is like an inheritance. It's been given to us. It's waiting for us. But we have to reach a certain level of maturity to experience the wealth. Yet, when it comes to spiritual matters, maturity isn't based on age or social standing or whether you marry a prince by the time you're twenty-one. It is measured by a person's openness to God.

If you have ever shared an intimate piece of yourself with a beloved, so that person can experience something you cherish, then you can understand with your mind and your heart why I wrote this book. I am not a theologian, nor am I a mystic or an intellectual. I am a beggar and I have been knocking outside God's door for some time now. I don't have much, but I would like to share with you the little bread I do have. Just a tiny crumb of it can transform your life.

I have borrowed some practices from Christian traditions—such as spiritual exercises and the Jesus Prayer, a simple yet powerful prayer—that have transformed not only my life, but the lives of millions of others throughout the centuries. This being said, *Exercising Your Soul* is not meant to be watered-down spirituality, but a book for the masses, a way of introducing readers to some unique spiritual practices that can bring you closer to God, Christ, and the Holy Spirit.

The exercises in this book are, I believe, a simple way to experience a certain type of union with God. Perfect union with God, as mystics and theologians have said over the years, happens in death. This doesn't mean we shouldn't try to get as close to God as humanly possible in our day-to-day lives. This is our calling. This is the intense desire that lies within our hearts, a yearning to connect with the divine.

The intention of this book is not to busy you with superfluous, unnecessary activity. Nor is it to make you a saint, though if it does, I think I get brownie points in heaven (and to be honest, I could use as many as I can get). The purpose of this book is to bring you to a greater awareness of God, who is already present in your life through the living Christ and the divine person of the Holy Spirit.

If a journey of a thousand miles begins with a single step, then I hope this book will serve as a pair of good walking shoes you put on before your feet even touch the ground. And if you are somewhere out there along the road already, in a town you never heard of, standing outside an all-night diner, catching a smoke, staring up at a black sky dotted with stars, I hope this book can be a touch of light reading that brings comfort between your arrivals and departures.

Part I

THE REASON WHY

The old man said this to the boy:

"Imagine for a moment that you are a newly created ship that is being unveiled to the world for the very first time. There is a lot of pomp and circumstance. There are celebrations. There is fanfare. Soon, someone comes along and whacks a champagne bottle against your backside and you slowly descend into the

water. You have been christened and you set off on the voyage of life.

"Now, you have good days and bad days. Some days are calm, others rage with storms. You are a solid ship—built with good materials and thoughtfully planned out—and you endure the placid seas as well as the thirty-foot swells.

"You are out on the ocean of life for years and overall you feel strong, but time has done what time does. It's aged you. You're weathered. The sun has helped to fade some of your luster. The salts of the sea have scratched you deeply and penetrated your surface. Many have walked across your decks—some with soft shoes, others with ten-pound clogs. You feel tired. Sometimes you even feel that a piece of you has died. When you feel this way it is time to make a journey back to dry dock, to the place where you were made, so that you can be restored.

"As you move into place and the water is drained all around you, it becomes obvious that your hull—your foundation—is covered in a thick layer of barnacles. Parasites. Your surface may have been worn down by exposure, but your base has been made inefficient by neglect. Looking at what was once your great hull, it is almost impossible to discern that you are a great and powerful ship. These hangers-on have slowed you down. In some ways they have protected you by covering up tiny holes that may have caused you to sink, but they are not part of who you are and, if left unattended, will cause more damage. These barnacles, these leeches, have slowed you on your journeys.

"The barnacles are scraped from your hull. The process is slow at first, slow and tedious. And painful. In time, you feel a great weight lifted from you. Rejuvenated, full of life, and you are ready to set sail on your next great voyage.

"It's like being born, but being born strong and powerful," said the old man.

"Is this why you are always praying to God?" asked the boy.

"Yes," said the old man. "So I can be scraped clean."

Chapter 1

WHITE RABBITS

D ID YOU KNOW that there are 1,440 minutes in a day? It's true. I did the math. Did you also know that 1 percent of all that time is fourteen minutes and twenty-four seconds? What would happen if you made a conscious decision, every day, to exercise your soul by giving roughly fifteen minutes of your time over to God? Just 1 tiny percent of your life. Would your life change?

Mine did.

From a very early age I had a deep desire to know God. Looking back on my life, I don't think this is surprising. I grew up in the shadow of a great twentieth-century cathedral, St. Agnes, by far one of the tallest structures on Long Island. I attended Catholic school for twelve years. And my mother was a bit of a suburban mystic, a woman who decorated our home with various illustrations of Jesus Christ and the Virgin Mary, bought us rosary beads for our birthdays, and talked of visions and saints and holy ghosts.

There was *God talk* all around me—at home, at school, at church, and even in dreams (I remember one recurring dream I had as a teenager where I asked Christ what the meaning of life was. He didn't tell me until years later). Still, for whatever reason, I just didn't *feel* a connection to this thing, this person, this God who was supposedly so important in our lives. In some ways, God was like an uncle I never met—the one in Canada with a drinking problem.

Everyone else seemed to know God. He was well liked. There were always stories to be told and photos around the house reminding me that he existed ("Look, here he is at a wedding with a glass of wine in his hand" or "This is a shot of him with all those children on his lap"), but I had absolutely no emotional connection to him.

God, who seemed so present for my mother, my grandmother, my teachers, was elusive to me. God was like a white rabbit. Not the white rabbit that Grace Slick and Jefferson Airplane sang about back in the sixties. Nor do I mean the white rabbit from *Alice's Adventures in Wonderland* (though we will see that living a spiritual life is a lot like falling into a certain kind of Wonderland). I mean the white rabbit I saw in the woods when I was twelve years old.

While I was growing up my family lived less than a mile from Hempstead Lake, one of only a few freshwater lakes on Long Island. When I was old enough to go off on my own, I would invariably ride my bike across town and go exploring in the woods around the lake. I don't know why, maybe it was an infatuation with King Arthur or the *Lord of the Rings,* but I always felt that I was going to hear a voice coming out of the lake or I would find a magic ring and take flight on a giant bubble to a faraway land. I enjoyed exploring, most of all during the autumn months when the land around the lake looked like daytime fireworks—explosions of red, yellow, and orange.

It was during one of these days wandering around alone in the woods that I saw something white flash in front of me. I stopped. I was frightened. Thinking about it now, I can still feel my heart pulsating in my left ear the way I did that day. I tried listening past my fear and heard crunching. It sounded like some kind of giant. I took a few steps to my right and soon had a clear view of the monstrosity!

A little white rabbit, his ears high, his nose twitching. He was munching on some kind of leaf. He was definitely not what I would call a giant.

I don't know what came over me because instantly I turned into some kind of gunless Elmer Fudd. I had one thought in my

head. *I'm going to catch this wascally wabbit!* I took a few steps toward this tiny scoundrel and we locked eyes. I took another step. The rabbit tensed its shoulders in front of me. I was midway through my next step when the rabbit darted faster than anything I had ever seen in my life. I ran after it, over fallen branches and layers of dry leaves. I don't remember how far I ran except that I quickly became winded and stopped. I remember bending over, my hands on my knees, panting and looking up and seeing the rabbit, still some distance away, staring back at me.

I took a deep breath. "I'm going to get you now," I said — and ran. The rabbit again took flight and darted deeper into the woods. I ran maybe another fifty feet and stopped. This happened again and again and the deeper I went into the big woods, the more afraid I became that I would never find my way out (walking through those woods now, I see I was never really more than a couple hundred feet from a road, but at the time it seemed like an endless vale). At a certain point I gave up and even though at the time there was nothing I desired more, I let the rabbit go. I looked around and slowly made my way back to a path that eventually led me back to the lake.

I have never forgotten that day in the woods, and over the years I've come to see that moment as a metaphor for my spiritual life. God was, in many ways, like that white rabbit. There was this mysterious, beautiful creature I wanted to capture and hold. I would run after it with all my might, only to become tired and discouraged when it would move away from me. No matter how hard I tried, God was always out of reach. I became convinced that God never wanted me to catch up. This was how I viewed the Almighty for most of my life: a quick-footed rabbit, a trickster — Bugs Bunny, only not as funny.

Then, a few years ago, I began to pray. I mean *really pray*. Not the half-hearted, going-through-the-motions kind of praying we do at church ("Dear God, you're great, but I'd rather be home sleeping"). Not the jabbering, making-deals-with-the-Almighty kind of praying ("Look, I know I'm not the most patient person in the world, but I promise to be really good if you let me kiss Mona Kenny, just once"), but serious, formal prayer, something I had never tried.

While I was growing up, prayer bored me, but now, the more I did it, the more it excited me. I soon began to realize that even though I was raised in a religious household and spent over a decade in Catholic schools, I was "prayer illiterate."

Within a short time, by praying just a few minutes every day, my life began to change and soon the rabbit in those autumnal woods began to slow down. I was getting a much better look at him. He was still mysterious, but now when I would set off in pursuit, the white rabbit that haunted my waking and sleeping moments for over ten years seemed willing to let me follow him. As I moved toward him, he would scamper off, but only a few feet. He would turn, stand, and face me, and I would follow. The rabbit wasn't running away from me. He was leading me to another place. It was soon thereafter that I realized God hadn't slowed down, *I had slowed down*. I had stopped running and that made all the difference.

Everything came alive for me. Things I had never noticed before began to take shape. I could now see the path I was on. I could smell the freshness of the trees around me. I could hear a world I never heard before. I could feel the air on my neck and for the first time in my life, I glimpsed the eyes of God.

I had been transformed.

*   *   *

What I realize now was that I had been suffering from a form of spiritual anorexia. Though I had grown up with religion all around me—and it was just about everywhere I went—I wouldn't let it enter into me. God, it now seemed, had been a banquet, but I had refused to eat. Something was keeping me away from nourishing my soul and in turn nourishing a relationship with God. My soul was hungry but I never opened my mouth.

Prayer soon led me to meditation and meditation soon led me back to prayer so that the two became entwined in my life in a way I never knew was possible. The more I spent time with God, the more I felt myself becoming stronger in my day-to-day life. This is not to say I wasn't weak—I had been asleep for over twenty years of my life and though any kind of spiritual muscle had atrophied to a point of almost becoming vestigial, with each minute I spent in prayer, I felt myself coming back to life. The scary thing is, for most of my life, I didn't even know I was dying.

After a few months of doing what I was calling "my daily 1 percent spiritual regimen" (prayer) followed by meditation, followed by prayer, followed by meditation—my vision started to change. By this, I don't mean I needed new glasses, but in many ways it was a bit like going to the eye doctor.

When you have your eyes examined, the ophthalmologist will put your head in a strange contraption, place lenses before your eyes, and ask you to read the letters you see on the wall across from you. She will then change the focus of the lens and ask you if the image is better or worse. Depending on how you answer she will change the focus again and again until you realize that the initial image, which seemed clear, was in fact quite blurry.

You had grown so used to living in an unfocused world that you didn't know better.

That's how I felt. I had been blind but now I could see—not fully, I was still spiritually legally blind—but I could see glimpses, colors, textures I had never seen before and it scared me.

In those weeks and months that followed, everywhere I looked I saw emaciated souls: in my friends, in my family, in my coworkers, and in the people on the street. On the surface most of these people were beautiful and smart and funny, but their spirits seemed unhealthy and in definite need of nourishment. This is not to say I considered myself anything special, but it helped me realize why so many people who seem to have so much going for them experience disillusionment and loneliness.

Every year millions of people spend thousands of dollars nurturing their bodies, exercising their muscles, supplementing their diets with vitamins and wonder drugs. Millions more people spend even more money exercising their minds by attending school in one form or another. Yet how many of those people spent a fraction of that time or money on exercising their souls every day? Certainly, some people do—the whole New Age, mind, body, spirit industry wouldn't exist if some people weren't out there doing yoga and meditating. But many Catholics and Christians, even the churchgoing ones, are still catching up to the idea that prayer and meditation should be—and need to be—a daily activity.

Most doctors recommend that you work out at least three days a week. Most students attend class at least five days a week. Yet many of us may attend a religious service once a week and think, *Well, that's done.* But that's not enough. Your cardiologist wouldn't say, "Hey Bill, look, I want you to run forty-five minutes on Sunday and then take the rest of the week off," would he?

*   *   *

Imagine this story. Once upon a time there was a young man who smoked a cigarette. It made him cough and choke, but something about it made him feel good, too. So he smoked another. Didn't cough as much this time. So he decided to try it a third time.

"Well, that was nice," he said. "I was feeling anxious before, but now I feel calm." He smoked some more and within a year he was up to three packs a day.

Ten years later the man is getting a checkup at his doctor's.

"Phil, you need to stop smoking."

"Why?"

"Because if you don't, you're going to die."

"Are you sure?"

"Phil, how many packs do you smoke a day?"

"Three."

Phil's doctor took out a prescription pad and started doing math: sixty cigarettes multiplied by 365 days multiplied by ten years. Phil, it seemed, had smoked 219,000 cigarettes in ten years' time. Over two hundred thousand cigarettes.

"You put smoke in your lungs almost a quarter of a million times, Phil."

He quit soon thereafter.

Most of us would agree that smoking is a bad habit. I think we can all agree that the physical size of a cigarette isn't that big, is it? It weighs very little and really, how long does one cigarette last? Five minutes? If you smoke two hundred thousand cigarettes in ten years and each cigarette last five minutes, you've spent over one million minutes of your life smoking. That's over sixteen thousand hours, nearly two full years of your life smoking cigarettes.

Many of us excel at cultivating bad habits, but what about a good habit? What about incorporating daily prayer and meditation in our lives? What if instead of smoking a cigarette you "smoked" a prayer or some form of spiritual exercise sixty times a day? That would mean smoking God for three hundred minutes a day. What would that do to the state of your soul? Don't be frightened. This book isn't about giving five hours to God, just fifteen tiny minutes.

But from small things, big things do come.

Chapter 2

WHAT IS A SPIRITUAL EXERCISE?

A SPIRITUAL EXERCISE is any practice that draws you closer to an experience of union with the divine. These practices could take the form of various types of prayer, meditation, or contemplation—three separate and distinct actions that are too often considered interchangeable.

In many ways spiritual exercises are like courting a beloved. You have a desire, a yearning for another and you suffer a gravitational pull to *do something*: touch, smell, listen, taste, to look upon this person who seems to be calling you from a place other than this strange, fragmented world we live in. When you and your beloved can't be together, for all the reasons that seem to keep lovers apart—distance, time, family, work—you spend your moments daydreaming, fantasizing, worshipping, writing love letters, seeking out gifts, scheduling times to meet alone, all in the hopes of surrendering in utter rapture with the other.

Yes, doing a spiritual exercise is like going on a date with God.

While spiritual exercises are common in many religions, many people associate the term with *Spiritual Exercises of Ignatius of Loyola,* a sort of military manual for the human soul, written by the Spanish theologian who founded the Jesuit order in 1540. Ignatius, a knight injured by a cannonball while defending Pamplona from the French, had a spiritual awakening shortly thereafter and pursued a course of theological exploration that led to his writing, which in turn transformed the way many of us approach a relationship with the Almighty.

Anyone who has tried to read through the *Spiritual Exercises,* though, knows it can be a daunting, albeit an important and gratifying, task. The information contained within that text can open windows to the soul that allow the warm, windy breath of the Holy Spirit to clear out spiritual rooms reeking of mothballs and stale experience.

Essentially, the exercises can lead to a greater awareness of the eternally alive God in the temporal experiences of our daily lives. Few books rival it in terms of importance in Christian spirituality. Yet the language Ignatius uses is dense and the practices are sometimes overly strenuous for the average person. Ignatius's *Spiritual Exercises* is sort of like James Joyce's *Ulysses*: a book many people talk about, but few people have read from cover to cover.

But what if you're a mom with very little time on your hands, or a father working two jobs to support your family, and you have a burning desire to know God, but very little time or patience to read through a sixteenth-century work written for members of a religious order?

In this book, I have loosely borrowed the idea of spiritual exercises from Ignatius and have incorporated some of his basic ideas—the importance of the imagination in prayer, meditation, and the reading of Scripture—into a book for the twenty-first-century reader.

That's right, for people with very little time on their hands.

Don't be fooled into thinking that simple things aren't difficult and complex at the same time. As Brother Lawrence, a French monk who lived nearly a hundred years after Ignatius, wrote in *Practicing the Presence of God*:

> We must be careful not to be deceived into thinking that this union is a simple expression of the heart, as in saying, "My God, I love You with all my heart," or other similar words. No, this union is something indefinable that is found in a gentle, peaceable, spiritual, reverent, humble, loving, and utterly simple soul. This "indefinable something" raises the soul and presses it to love God, to worship Him and yes, even to caress Him with an inexpressible tenderness known only to those who experience it.

We as human beings are attracted to the unknown. Many of us fall in love less with the known aspects of an individual than with the mystery that lies beyond the seen. Yes, on the surface I can fall in love with a smile or a laugh, but those things are just signposts to something else—a fiery desire to hear an orchestra of angels in the eyes of a beloved, to see the colors of music in a long-awaited, hoped-for arrival, to taste the tongue of the divine in the whispered embrace of a departure.

It is in this unknown that we find a connection that binds us to God and to each other. This connection is none other than the

Holy Spirit. Some things exist beyond ourselves. God, however, is not one of them. Some of us may accept this intellectually—that the Spirit of God lives in each and every one of us—but it is the objective of this book to move away from the mind, to stop thinking, and to descend, not into nothingness, but to the depths of *everythingness,* a place where every thing, every person, every moment, every desire, every yearning is connected to each other and all those things are connected to God. It is a place of perpetual prayer, a place where you no longer *practice* the presence of God, you *experience* that presence fully in body and soul—two components of our existence that are intricately woven together.

This is the heart of the spiritual life.

When many of us talk about spiritual matters, there tends to be an "easier said than done" sword of Damocles stationed above our heads that keep us from taking the step forward. *Oh, I'd like to spend more time with God, but I'm just too busy. Oh, I just can't sit still for that long. Oh, it's boring. Oh, I tried and it was just too difficult for me. Oh, what good is prayer going to do anyway?*

Living a spiritual life is not difficult. Certainly *it can be,* the way walking from a living room to a kitchen can be difficult if I decided to throw my legs in the air and walk on my hands. I, like you, am created in God's image, but I am no acrobat. I would certainly fall on my tailbone and do some serious damage to my body. To make matters worse, my wife would laugh at me and call me names as she spoon-fed me minced carrots in a hospital room.

No, living a spiritual (or prayerful) life can be as simple as drinking a glass of water. If you are blessed to have a relatively sound body and mind, and equally blessed to live in a home with clean running water, it's really as easy as *realizing* you're thirsty, deciding to take action, and then standing up from your chair, walking to the kitchen, taking a glass off your shelf, turning on the faucet, and drinking. *Ah, refreshing. I didn't realize I was that thirsty. Let me have another.*

The spiritual life can be that way too. I felt thirsty. I decided I needed some water. I took a drink. Wow, was I actually starting to turn to sand? I had no idea.

This does not mean that leading a spiritual life does not require effort on our part, but I can assure you, as someone who has grown into a spiritual life, that a little goes a very long way. In many instances, all it takes are small changes in your life. A single prayer has more power than you ever thought possible.

Maybe you're afraid that people will think you're weird. Look, you don't even have to tell anyone what you're doing. You can let it be a secret between you and God. In time, though, people will begin noticing a change coming over you—a positive change. Actions, they say, speak louder than sermons. Folks might think you've lost weight or comment on how less stressed you look (and you will lose emotional and spiritual weight that has kept you from ascending to the type of person God intended you to be).

This also does not mean that once you embark on a spiritual life that you won't encounter difficulty. Spiritual living doesn't make you immune to the troubles of life, but it does give you strength. With the power of the Holy Spirit, these exercises, like physical exercises, will make you stronger.

Imagine for a moment that there are two people standing on a tree branch ten feet above the ground. Both people are of equal height and weight. Yet one person is physically fit while the other person is out of shape. They have the same body mass, only one has muscle and the other person has flab. Do you have that picture in your mind?

Now, kick them both off the tree at the same time, using equal force in your kick. Both victims, in our little imagining, hit the ground at the same time. Gravity, it seems, does not play favorites.

Which one suffers fewer injuries?

The answer?

Well, it's a trick question. They both suffer sprained ankles.

But which one recovers faster?

The person who was physically fit, that's who. The out-of-shape person ends up suffering pain in his tendon for the rest of his days.

The same is true of the spiritual life. All of us will experience moments of joy and sorrow, ease and struggle, loneliness and elation, whether it be at the birth or death of a loved one, a new job that turns out to not be what you expected, disappointments in friendships, financial insecurities, the devastations caused by war. Difficulties do not go away when one undertakes the spiritual journey.

In fact, the road to spiritual fitness can be wild and overrun by brush and thorns. There is the likelihood of getting cut. In most cases, leading a spiritual life means struggle because as you begin to turn your focus more and more to God, the more you realize that the life you were living wasn't much of a life at all. Yet, as you go on, you will have the strength to face these challenges in a courageous way. And if injuries do occur while you are walking—and sometimes running—on this path, you'll be able to recover faster and not be deterred from your goal.

That goal?

Union with God.

There are other reasons people are afraid of living a life of the Spirit. For one, many people think they need to *totally* renounce their way of living right now. Now, I am not a priest or a theologian, but I vehemently disagree. Obviously, if you're a serial killer, you should stop now, but few of us are homicidal maniacs and little in our lives happens instantaneously. For most of us, change happens glacially. It's seems that the glaciers that existed ten thousand years ago took a long time to move to the ocean, but the landscapes they left in their wake are truly amazing.

Far too many of us approach the spiritual life "with too little patience," Karol Wojtyla (Pope John Paul II) wrote in his book *The Way to Christ*, "as if it were a matter of something like a surgical operation or an injection, which will immediately make us better again. Change is a long-term process."

What frightens people away from a fitness plan, whether it's physical or spiritual, is fear of the short-term negative impact on their lives. I am a firm believer that people are not afraid of change itself. If I said to you, "I'm going to transform your life by giving you a million dollars," would you fear that? You might be afraid I had recently escaped from Bellevue, or that the money I have to give you was stolen from a Wall Street robber baron. But if everything was legitimate, you'd do cartwheels.

On the other hand, if I said to you, "I'm going to install a new complicated computer system at your job that's going to make your life difficult and will take you twice as long to do your work," you're going to start shaking. People don't fear change. They fear their lives are going to be worse off than they were before the change. Change in many ways needs to happen in spoonfuls.

Where does this idea of total renunciation come from? Blame the saints for this notion that drastic change needs to happen overnight. They ruined it for everyone. They are a bit like those people at work with perfect attendance records. Imagine that you want to stay home because you have the flu but you feel obligated to drag your weary body out of bed because Kenny, the associate manager, who was hit by a bus on the way to work last week, still managed to get to the office later that afternoon. He had two broken legs and a concussion, but he just couldn't miss that 3:30 PM meeting about cleaning out the office refrigerator on Fridays.

Kenny always ruins it for everyone.

So, too, do the saints. Saint Francis renounced his wealth and his businessman father and began hanging out with the destitute and with the furry woodland creatures (Thanks, Frank, for making me feel bad for having borrowed that money from my dad when I was twenty to get a car, and for my dislike of squirrels). Or then there is Saint Stephen who took some arrows to the chest for Christ (if I get a hangnail I'm a huge baby. I need ibuprofen and a nap). Or Saint Peter who was crucified upside down (I won't even begin to tell you about the vertigo I get when I bend my neck a certain way). Or Mother Teresa (she's not a saint, but she should be one) and the millions of people she helped around the world. Or Martin Luther King Jr. (he's not a saint either but I vote for him as well). But how does anyone live up to those legacies?

These are extreme examples, and while these lives were dramatic, bold, and honorable, what many of us see in these people are *the culminations of lives lived spiritually* and not the small steps — and granted, sometimes, giant leaps of faith — it took to get there.

One last reason people seem to stay away from leading a spiritual life can be seen in this little imagining:

Have you ever watched *Family Feud*? It's a TV game show where two families face off in order to win a lot of money. One member from each family meets the host at a center podium and a question is asked. The first person to slap the red turtle-shell-like buzzer wins the right to answer the question. If the person who hits first answers incorrectly, the member from the opposing family has his shot at glory. Let's imagine for a moment that I'm a contestant on the show and my opponent is Nathanial McAngryPants. Nate is a little high-strung and needs more fiber in his diet.

"One hundred people were surveyed," says our host. Let's say for this scenario it's the legendary kissing host, Richard Dawson. "Here's the question: name something people are."

As I'm thinking, *Well, that's not a question, it's a more like a request,* my game-show nemesis slaps the buzzer like a proud West Kentucky farmer slapping the backside of his prized Holstein at a county fair.

"Jerks!" McAngryPants exclaims.

"Show us 'jerks'!" our fine host calls out.

The buzzer bleats and a big X appears out of nowhere.

Where did that big red X come from? I'm asking myself. Without skipping a beat our well-trained and oh-so-professional host turns to me and after a few seconds of squinting and furling my forehead so the space between my eyes looks like an old man's lips after sucking a lemon, I shrug my shoulders and say, "Tired?" I answered his statement with a question. I'm not sure this is allowed, but the judges let it go that day.

"Show us 'tired'!"

Ding, ding, ding!

"You have control of the board" are the last words I hear before Nathanial McAngryPants leaps over the podium and grabs me by my muttonchops (I've always wanted to grow a pair of muttonchops, but I can barely grow a beard and since this is my imagining, I have them) and yells, "Jerks!"

I'm not a statistician and I did not survey one hundred people for this information (though if there had been a narcolepsy convention near my home I certainly would have), but if I had to make an educated guess about one thing I think most people are, it's tired. I know I'm tired. You're probably tired, too, and if you say you're not, it's probably because you're too tired to admit it. Some of us are tired physically. Others of us are tired mentally. Most of us, it seems, are tired spiritually.

We may be tired of our families, our friends, our jobs. We may be tired of waiting at the same red light every day on the way to school. We may be tired of our neighbors. We may be tired of crime in our neighborhoods or tired of never catching a break. We may be tired because no matter how hard we try we can't save any money. We may be tired of the same old news we hear every day: the world is at war, terrorism is on the rise, murder is happening everywhere, the economy is failing, our leaders are idiots, and the movie star you admire so much is a bad tipper.

We may be tired because no matter how hard we try, we can't lose weight. We may be tired because of an illness. Tired because someone we love is spiraling out of control because of an addiction. We may be tired of our children not listening to us. We might be tired of feeling isolated, of feeling alone, or of feeling weak. Tired of being frustrated, disappointed, moody, irritable, broken. We may be tired that no matter how hard we pray we never hear God speaking to us.

Tiredness is one of the biggest culprits that keep people away from the spiritual life. Prayer and meditation are a surefire way of energizing you. They're even better than Red Bull and Pop Rocks. And while many people believe that what they are looking for in their lives is rest—Saint Augustine's often quoted "We are restless, Lord, until we find rest in you" comes to mind—when we turn our lives to God, rest is the very last thing we could want. And if you don't believe me, what happens every time the Holy Spirit makes an appearance in the New Testament?

Someone takes action.

We are at rest, Lord, until we wake up and take action in you.

Awareness is key.

It's not as if God isn't with us now. It's just that we don't see him. It is in many ways like the gargoyle with the outstretched neck on the facade of the church down the street from where I grew up. Yes, it was something that frightened and awed me as a child, but as I grew older I'd forgotten it was even there. Then a friend of mine, visiting from another state, said as we were walking down the block, "Look up there! How strange and wonderful!"

Yes, God is present in you. How strange. How wonderful.

Ultimately, to live a spiritual life all it takes is a slight shift of our focus. Certainly the *Titanic* could have been saved from disaster if it had shifted its direction when leaving port by a single degree south. A single degree.

What changes would happen in our lives if we shifted our focus by a single degree? What would happen to us if we made just a tiny little change in our lives and gave just fifteen minutes daily to exercising our souls by giving that time to God? That's just

1 percent, the other 99 percent you can do whatever you want with. Want to find out?

Come. It is time for you to step forward and redefine what it means to be human in the eyes of God by seeing God in all things. It's time to strengthen that soul of yours.

Wait. What is a soul? Good question.

Chapter 3

SOULS, MUSTARD SEEDS, AND REDEFINING HUMANITY

ACCORDING TO theologian John A. Hardon, a soul is "the spiritual immortal part in human beings that animates their bodies."

Awesome!

But what does that mean?

Keeping that definition in mind, please consider that the soul isn't some dry intellectual concept, but a vibrant, energizing, electrifying component of our lives. The soul is not complete in itself—it needs to give life to a body. It is, however, the part of us that gives our existence meaning.

The soul is, in many ways, like an electric frying pan. It's connected to an energy source. The pan is at different times cold, warm, or hot. It takes the individual ingredients of our lives— our joys, our sorrows, our disappointments, our questions; the people, the places, the things; our relationships; our bodies, sensations, and emotions—and cooks them. It brings all these pieces of our lives together. Salt is added and everything coalesces into a something new. No longer do we have a bunch of heated, separate ingredients, we have a meal.

What does a meal do? It nourishes us. It gives us strength. It transforms us. It brings people together. It satisfies a hunger.

In this metaphor, God is our source, the heat and the salt that brings out our essence (for those who can't have sodium, God is Mrs. Dash), and through the gift of free will, we control the degree to which our lives—that is, our meals—are formed. The trick, as in cooking, is knowing what the right temperature should be. Cook your food at too low a temperature and you end up waiting years for it to gel. By that time, everyone has either ordered takeout or has gone to sleep. Cook your food at too high a temperature and you chance burning and a visit from your local firefighters, who aren't going to be too happy when they see that the purported four alarm was really some burnt turkey and bean chili.

Balance, it seems, is key. Many of us know this. As with Icarus, flying too high and too close to the sun means you burn and crash; fly too low near the water and your wings are weighed down and you drown. Yet, in our attempt to find a middle ground, we resign ourselves to living lukewarm lives. We don't sin in major ways and we don't do good in major ways either.

In Dante's *Inferno,* the lukewarm are some of the most wretched of the damned and in the New Testament, the lukewarm are spit out of God's mouth. I am absolutely not advocating sin, but there is a certain boldness—granted, a misdirected boldness—in the actions of all great sinners. The problem seems to be an ultimate faith in oneself, a person who dares to act above universal law—God's law. The error isn't in the actual boldness, it's in the focus. Instead of acting boldly and lovingly in the name of the Father, we act boldly in the names of ourselves. The error, again, lies in where we shift our attention.

What is hate except a shifting of our focus away from love? What is despair, but shifting our focus away from hope? What is anger except a shifting away from forgiveness? And what are we when we shift our attention away from God?

Too many of us trying to lead good lives end up playing it safe. We shift our focus to our own abilities to keep us secure. And if you're playing it safe, how much faith in God do you really have?

We are not called to be sinners. Nor are we are called to be lukewarm, wet, onion-like transparencies of God's greatest creation. We are called by Christ to be bold, courageous human beings infused with the Holy Spirit. We are called to be heroic. We are called to be miracle workers. "I tell you the truth, anyone who has faith in me will do what I have been doing. He will do even *greater things* than these" (John 14:12; italics added).

Human history has stolen the human being and covered it under thousands of years of fighting, wars, and bloodshed. It is like a jewel covered in mud. Spiritual exercises—daily, directed prayer and meditation—strengthen our faith, and that increased power of belief, in turn, helps us to grow closer to God.

You may be thinking, *How could something as small as a prayer do all that?* If I were a well-seasoned jazz musician, I'd reply, "It's all about mustard seeds, baby." Since I'm a suburban mall rat, I'll just drop the "baby" and say, "It's all about mustard seeds."

The kingdom of heaven is like a mustard seed, which a man took and planted in his field. Though it is the smallest of all your seeds, yet when it grows, it is the largest of garden plants and becomes a tree, so that the birds of the air come and perch in its branches.

(Matthew 13:31–32)

I tell you the truth, if you have faith as small as a mustard seed, you can say to this mountain, "Move from here to there" and it will move. Nothing will be impossible for you. *(Matthew 17:20)*

I remember the first time I heard the parable of the mustard seed. It was around the time of my First Communion. My teacher was a feisty old crow who cared less for the state of our souls and more about the state of our fingernails. She had some obsession with checking our fingernails for dirt. Every day we all had to walk up to her desk and show our hands. She would check for clean hands and then raise our fingers to her bifocaled eyes and examine under our nails.

Maybe she was a frustrated forensic scientist, I don't know. But if the cleanliness of my hands was any indication of the cleanliness of my soul, well, mine was tainted black and muddy (I liked to play in the dirt a lot then—still do). I thought she was the nastiest woman I had ever met, and I think the feeling was mutual since every day I would get hollered at for not having clean hands. I do remember scrubbing them and then washing them daily before I went to school, but somewhere along the way they'd get all dirty again.

Anyway, after one particular examination, she screamed at me, "If you only gave a mustard-seed amount of effort toward washing your hands, you'd have the cleanest hands in the world!"

"What's a mustard seed?" I asked. I knew mustard was

something for hot dogs, but I never knew there was a seed. Other children in the classroom chimed in: "What is a mustard seed?"

She then told us all to get into a circle and she told us a story. As much as she was a clean-hand militant, Ms. Snyder was a pretty good storyteller. She told us Jesus' parable and when it was over, the words "If you have the faith of a mustard seed, you can move mountains" circled inside my head.

"I can move mountains?" I asked her.

"Not you. You can't even keep your hands clean."

I felt as if I was going to cry and I think she felt bad because she changed her tone. "Well, maybe you can, when you get older—if you have enough faith."

This was amazing! I was a big-time reader of comic books and I had asked my parents for years whether people could really fly, if they had superhuman strength and could pick up buildings, if they could use a power ring and create anything that was in their minds, if they had super speed. The answer was always no, but here was my teacher, my fingernail Nazi, telling me that one day I might be able to move mountains.

So, I started training. I was going to move mountains.

Well, my first attempt at moving a mountain came during church one day when I tried moving a statue with my mind. I remember focusing on the statue and repeating to myself, *I have faith, now move. I have faith, now move.* I looked up and, well, nothing happened. This did not deter me. *Obviously, I need more training.* Even though a mustard seed seemed awfully small to me, I knew deep down I wasn't the best kid in the world. I was always getting into trouble at home and in school and my hands—well, I just couldn't get over the whole washing thing—but still I dreamt of moving mountains.

This went on for years. Sometimes I would forget about

the story, and other times I would go on these so-called training binges where I would focus on something and try to make it move. I may not have liked Ms. Snyder, but I thought she was always honest with me. In the quiet of my room, I would sit and pray and usually fall asleep. I tried levitating myself once and fell down a flight of stairs.

Some years later, I found myself in Denver for a conference. My faith had waxed and waned over the years, but I was feeling pretty strong spiritually and since this was the first time I was going to see a tried-and-true mountain, I was going to put my faith to use.

So, I rented a car and within five minutes drove into the mountains, which in Denver means driving a block or two, and I pulled over at the side of the road and stood there, looking at a grand, snowcapped Goliath.

"Today, you meet your match, O Large One." (Even as I got older, I spoke in comic book language.) "It is I, David." (I didn't speak my real name out loud because I didn't want to get in trouble in case I started an earthquake.) "My slingshot is my faith. You will move, mountain."

By this time in my life, my early twenties, I felt pretty confident. I was convinced that I had faith at least the size of a baseball. Okay, maybe a golf ball, but it was definitely bigger than a mustard seed.

"Move, mountain, move," I said.

Nothing.

I closed my eyes.

"Move, mountain, move! Move, mountain, move!"

I kept repeating the phrase for at least five minutes and, well, *I started to feel something.* I started to feel something well up inside me and I could feel my feet start to tingle.

"Move, mountain, move!"

Each time I said those words now, I felt stronger and stronger. I felt as if I were just about to strike oil, that I had my feet planted firmly in the ground and I was drilling into the tectonic plates and I was going to move this mountain. I was convinced! My faith was unstoppable.

I repeated the words one more time: "Move, mountain, move!" I opened my eyes!

Nothing happened.

I think, but I'm not 100 percent sure, that a bird crapped on my shoulder. Stupid bird.

I stared up at that mountain and that mountain stared back at me. "Mustard seed," it seemed to say to me. "Yeah, sure. Go home, kid."

Well, this crushed me and I have to admit my faith was shaken by this incident. I didn't stop believing in God, but I started putting limits on what I believed. The parables, for instance, stopped being living truths for me, they became nice stories. They expressed interesting ideas, but they were just that—ideas, nothing else.

Fairy tales.

Well, ten years passed and my spiritual journey took many twists and turns and I must have come back to that story I loved so much when I was younger because one morning I awoke and realized that the story was true! It was true! I was like Ebenezer Scrooge on Christmas morning. Somewhere overnight I had had an awakening and the story was true! And it had been proven in the twentieth century!

It wasn't a priest or a pope or a mystic or Mother Teresa who proved that the story of the mustard seed was legitimate. It was scientists. Einstein. Fermi. Oppenheimer. Atomic physicists! These people believed in something the size of a mustard seed. Actually, they believed in something smaller than a mustard seed, something they couldn't even see—the atom.

These scientists were able to harness the power of the atom. They were able to take something so infinitesimally small and unleash its energy. In the process they created something more powerful than anything human beings had ever created.

The atom bomb.

From one atom, something smaller than a mustard seed, scientists now had enough power to seismically move a mountain. Not only could they shake a mountain, they could destroy one.

Now if you and I are made up of a billion tiny atoms, how much God-given potential—how much God-given power—lies inside each and every one of us? Not to destroy. Not to annihilate mountains, but to move the things in our lives that block us from being truly human and to raise, through the power of the Holy Spirit and the grace of God, ourselves and others to new life in union with God.

How do we do this? Well, we can't. God does it through us, but prayer and meditation allow us to knock on God's door so he can answer and allow the gift of human potential—the gift of first life he bestowed on Adam—to flow through us.

We were not created to be flawed creatures. We were called by God to greatness. As much as I love my Christian and Catholic faith, too much time has been spent focusing on how vile human beings are. We need to shift that focus. I'm not saying to ignore sin, but when you focus on something you become that thing. If I focus in my mind on the idea that I'm a loser, I will become a loser. If I focus on becoming a great student, I will become a great student.

Yet, somehow we believe that two thousand years of focusing on sin will make us not sin. Hmmm. Who was the marketing genius that came up with that one? The devil's greatest power isn't possessing someone's soul. It's distraction.

In 1843, Nathaniel Hawthorne, the author of *The Scarlet Letter*, published a short story called "The Birthmark." At the center of this tale is a beautiful young woman with a tiny hand-shaped birthmark on her face. She is the talk of the town, praised for her beauty and desired by many. There is one young man, a scientist, who falls for the gorgeous young woman, courts her, and eventually marries her. After their wedding, the young man becomes obsessed with his wife's birthmark and as the days wear on he begins to see her as ugly, a perfect being marred by this hideous defect. Soon the young woman buys into her husband's opinion and considers herself an abomination.

The young scientist decides he can create a way to get rid of the mark and make this near-perfect creature perfect. He gives her a potion to drink. She drinks and the mark fades. The young man has gained what he has always wanted: perfection.

Minutes later his wife dies, and the love of his life is lost forever.

Each of us has a birthmark. This mark is very real and can be very dangerous, but over the last two thousand years the focus has been less on the beauty of the creation and more on the defect. How many of us grew up hearing more about sin and less about love?

I'm not saying that we're not sinful creatures. I can speak only for myself, but my soul looks as if it's been working in a Pennsylvania coal mine for decades. Yet, many of us act like a person who owns a beautiful diamond but focuses only on the tiny scratch deep within. There are few perfect diamonds in the world. Each has a flaw. We have spent the whole of human history focusing not on the radiance of the diamond, but obsessing on the blemish. Instead of focusing on love and forgiveness, we've nursed anger and hatred (and those twins have become some really unruly children).

God created us to be greater than the angels! *Greater than the angels!* We slipped and fell and scratched ourselves. The cut, the bleeding, however, does not change our original nature. Instead the enemy has shifted our focus ever so slightly away from the forgiving beauty of God to depravity. If we become what we focus on, then we as *human beings have become everything we were never intended to be.*

Think of it this way. You're driving on the highway, minding your own business, admiring the beautiful sky in front of you. You're keeping up with traffic and then, out of the corner of your eye, you see a big, naked, ugly, hairy man running on the side of the road giving everyone a thumbs-up. You can't take your eyes off this crazy guy and in the process your car veers into the next lane and you get into an accident with someone who was so shocked by the big hairy naked guy that she didn't know what to do either.

Sin is a big, hairy, chaffy naked guy. We focus more on that than on God, the Giver of love and life, and that big, bold beautiful sky in front of us. What happens when we shift our focus?

We crash.

Prayer and meditation will help you to steal back what it means to be truly human. What does it mean to be truly human? To live knowing that God, through the living person of the Holy Spirit, is inside you and inside everyone else, too. To live, to truly live is to see God in everything.

Everything.

Chapter 4

PRAYER, MEDITATION, AND CONTEMPLATION

L ET'S TAKE a few moments to talk specifically about prayer and meditation, as well as something we haven't really touched upon but is the fruit of both: contemplation. Many people use these three words interchangeably, but while there are similarities between them, there are subtle and not-so-subtle differences between the three that, once understood, can lead to a deepening of your spiritual life.

Prayer, John A. Hardon says, is our "voluntary response to the awareness of God's presence." Essentially, prayer is talking to God, either verbally, mentally, or physically, and can take many different forms including:

Petitionary: Asking for something
Adoration: Praising God
Thanksgiving: Expressing gratitude
Expiation: Asking specifically for mercy

Centering: Focusing on a single representative word for God
Mental and meditative: Using the mind to engage God in
    thought
Contemplative: Gazing on God without words

Prayer can take other forms as well. It can be solitary or done within a community. It can be a letter written to God. It can be a poem or a song or a dance. It can be an outstretched hand helping someone across the street or soothing a young child. It can be your job.

It all depends on your intention. Are you using your actions to communicate with God?

The premise of this book is to practice certain types of formal prayer so that you move toward a state of living in perpetual prayer.

Prayer is a gift from God for our benefit and is a way of entering into a state of intimacy. Practically speaking, it is a tool that helps relieve stress and anxiety, quiet our minds, center our souls, and lead more efficient lives.

I grew up in a house that was well over eighty years old. This house had a series of cast-iron radiators to keep the house warm. During the winter months, the furnace would kick in and the heat and pressure would move the warmed water through the pipes and heat the house.

Every year, though, we had to bleed the air from the pipes, which means we had to open the valves in the radiators to let out all the air that had accumulated in the spring and summer when the heating system wasn't in use. It's a pretty simple thing to do. You start the furnace and then at each radiator you use a special key to open a pressure valve that lets out all the air inside the pipes. If you didn't bleed your pipes every year it could make for a very dangerous situation. Worst case scenario: pipes with air in their systems can clang and shake, which can lead to bursting and water damage. Even if it's not that severe, the system will run inefficiently.

Prayer is a lot like bleeding your pipes. You are a powerful, wonderful creation and God wants you to run as smoothly as possible. Sometimes things don't function correctly. Pockets of discontent and doubt can creep into your system and, once pressure is applied, it can make you buckle, shake, and sometimes pop. Prayer allows you to open the valve, to let the air out so that the steam of the Holy Spirit can flow through you in a continuous stream. The more you pray, the more efficient you become in your life.

If prayer is speaking to God, meditation, on the other hand, is essentially, as Richard Foster says in *Celebration of Discipline*, "listening to God." Meditation is listening to God's voice. It also helps us to move away from an "it's all about me" inclination and allows us to cultivate a healthy amnesia of self. It is the beginning and the continuation of prayer.

God calls us. We respond. We listen. We respond. We listen. And so on. It's a bit like a dance. God leads. We follow.

Christian meditation, which differs from eastern meditation, is less about emptying ourselves and more about allowing God to fill us with his desires for us. When we pray we are usually expressing our needs to God. Meditation allows God to tell us his desires. "What happens in meditation," Foster writes, "is that we create the emotional and spiritual space which allows Christ to construct an inner sanctuary of the heart.... Meditation opens the door and, although we are engaging in specific meditative exercises at specific times, the aim is to bring this living reality into all of life."

Yet many of us may have tried meditation and never heard anything. Not one peep from God. Not a word. Not even a clearing of the throat or a sneeze.

Many have written that God speaks in silence. Well, that's great, but that doesn't do me much good. How do I know if God is there if his native tongue is *silencio?*

Experts who study human relationships estimate that nearly 80 percent of all communication is nonverbal. For instance, a friend asks your opinion about the guy she's dating. She says she really wants your viewpoint. So, you say, "Sure," and you let it rip, but as soon as you start talking, your friend folds her arms, tightens her jaw, and smiles a smile that if smiled by a baby would mean his diaper needed changing.

As you continue speaking, she keeps nodding and saying, "Thank you, I needed to hear this." That's what her mouth is saying, but what is her body saying? She hates you and she wants you to shut up.

If so much of the way we communicate is nonverbal, couldn't God be communicating to us nonverbally? Meditation therefore helps us understand God's body language. How can we read this? By reading the signs of God's creation around us, by listening to the voices of others and paying attention to how those words affect us emotionally and intellectually. Few of us are ever going to hear God speak in dramatic tones. Most of the time his words come from places you'd never expect—a friend, a bird, a song on your iPod, a billboard, a pothole, an illness, a disappointment— and when it does, you are on your way to contemplative experience of God.

Not too long ago I was in need of some serious inspiration. I was praying and meditating and nothing, absolutely nothing, was happening and I was getting very frustrated. I had heard that a favorite priest of mine was back from a long trip to Poland and I was excited to hear him preach on the upcoming Sunday. I'm not exaggerating when I say that I waited anxiously all week to listen to his words, which always brought me comfort and inspiration.

Sunday finally arrived and I was sitting in the pew eagerly anticipating the homily. Just as the priest finished reading the gospel and started to preach, a baby two rows behind me started to cry.

The infant didn't stop.

This baby had some set of lungs. I remember turning and looking at the parents as if to say, "Please take your spawn and leave! Some of us need to listen to this guy." Coward that I am, I said nothing and just tried to listen through the screaming.

I couldn't pay attention to the priest. I tried. I really did, but I couldn't hear anything except the wail of this child.

I started to get angry and, God forgive me, an instant of hate flashed into my heart. All I wanted to do was to get out of the spiritual dark place I was in and my one salvation was this homily. I couldn't make out a single word.

When the priest was done, guess what? Yes, the baby stopped crying.

I left church soon thereafter. Dejected and angry.

That night I had a dream.

In this dream, I was standing before Jesus (or at least my image of Jesus—he looked a little bit like Michael Landon with a beard) and I asked him, "What is the meaning of life?"

Christ looked at me, smiled, opened his mouth, and out came a cry of a baby.

I woke up.

I wasn't in church that day to hear God in the priest's voice. I was there to hear God in the cries of a child.

That moment after waking wasn't an intellectual knowing, it was an emotional experiencing of God. It was a feeling. As I lay in the dark of the night I felt strange. I felt changed, but I couldn't tell you how. Only after reflecting the next day did I realized that upon awakening, I had walked through the door to contemplation.

There are several distinct definitions of contemplation. Many times the word is confused with meditation. In the secular sense, this is fine, but in Christian spirituality, the two are very different. According to our friend Hardon, Saint Augustine called contemplation the enjoyable admiration of perceived truth, Saint Bernard defined it as the elevation of the mind resting on God, and Saint Thomas believed it to be a simple divine truth that produces love. In his book, *New Seeds of Contemplation,* Thomas Merton offers his own explanation:

[Contemplation] is the highest expression of man's intellectual and spiritual self.... It is spiritual wonder. It is spontaneous awe at the sacredness of life, of being. It is gratitude of life, for awareness and for being. It is a vivid realization of the fact that life and being in us proceed from an invisible, transcendent and infinitely abundant Source. Contemplation is, above all, awareness of the reality of that Source.

In its essence, contemplation is an experience of God that comes from God. It's something ineffable and to try to put it into words will always end in disappointment (which doesn't mean we shouldn't try). And though you can prepare yourself for contemplation by praying and meditating, you cannot force contemplation to occur.

You and I can pray. We can pray together. We can pray alone. We can pray with our minds or with our bodies. We can say words or we can be silent. We can also meditate and relax the body. These are things we can work out. These are exercises we can do. Contemplation, on the other hand, can't be *done*. It's something that happens to us.

It is a gift from God.

Contemplation is grace.

Part II

THE PRAYER EXERCISES

The old man spoke:

"You are like a person who has waited his entire life to see a painting in a museum. You finally get your chance to travel, to go to this place you have been dreaming about. You enter, you find where the painting is, and you walk to the room. Before you enter, you take a deep breath and then walk in. The painting is to the right and you automatically move as close to it as you possibly can without touching it. Certainly if the security guard was paying attention, you would be told to step away. But you are here.

You are looking at the painting you have waited your whole life to see and you can see the gentle curves of the brush, the color of a patch of the piece. You are so close you can even see the scarcely perceptible fingerprints of the artist that are barely distinguishable from the brushstroke.

"Something catches your eye, though, and you turn around and see another man, a distinguished and gentle man standing in the middle of the room observing the same painting as you are, but from a distance. He must be viewing you, too, because you've become a part of the painting yourself, you're so close to it. You are intrigued and you want to see what he sees, so you move closer to him. Standing shoulder to shoulder (you're a bit shorter than he is), you look around and you see the painting you've always wanted to see, but from a different perspective. It is beautiful, but so are all these other paintings that you missed in the room."

Chapter 5

LEARNING TO LISTEN

THIS BOOK attempts to explain, through definition and personal reflections, certain types of prayer and offers some guided meditations that will hopefully prepare you for an experience of God.

However, we do not have control over how God will respond to us. Some of us may pray, not just for fifteen minutes a day, but for hours during the day, and never have God respond to us the way we want him to. There is only one guarantee in the spiritual life: *God wants us to experience him in this life; we just don't have control over how this is going to happen.* We can, though, be diligent in our faith and till the soil of our hearts and souls to make them fertile ground for the seed of God's love to take root.

Furthermore, this book is not a comprehensive lexicon on prayer and meditation. It leans heavily toward three types of prayer: breath, centering, and Lectio Divina (praying with Scripture). I have spotlighted these three because I believe we live in a world of great thinkers. By this I don't mean that everyone is a pocket-protected rocket scientist or a pipe-smoking, tweed-wearing intellectual philosopher, rather that humans are always thinking. We may be thinking about God or we may be thinking about a bill we need to pay. We may be thinking of someone we love or plotting revenge against an enemy. We think about our health, our jobs, the economy, our car in need of brakes, whether or not we should buy new shoes or paint our house. For most of us, if we're not speaking with our mouths, we're rambling in our heads.

While thinking is important, too much of it, focused on the wrong things, can lead to depression, anger, and jealousy. As a society, as a race, we all need to stop thinking so much. Breath prayer, centering, and Lectio Divina can help us silence the mind and relax the body.

In addition I have interspersed personal reflections and short exercises that I hope will assist you with your prayer journey.

None of these prayers and exercises will take more than a couple of minutes to perform (some will take only a matter of seconds), but in order to become spiritually proficient, you must use the art of repetition daily. A great baseball pitcher doesn't throw a ball once a day. He throws it hundreds of times. A dancer doesn't practice a five-second move two minutes a day, she does it over and over again. You have life not because your heart beats once, but because it repeats that action over and over again.

Before we move on, just a few words on spiritual dryness and boredom.

There are going to be moments when you feel absolutely nothing on your spiritual journey. Frustration can follow. Anger can follow as well. You may become uninterested and fed up. Do not fall into this trap. Just as a person can walk around during a cloudy day and still return home with a sunburn, there will be times when you do not feel the effects of spiritual exercises. This does not mean they are not working. This is where real faith comes into play. It's easy to have faith when we feel God is speaking to us, when we're excited about the journey and what we might discover, but the true test of faith is when God is silent and we grow confused over what that silence means.

Recently a book was published by Mother Teresa. It was a posthumous collection of her writings that describe how alienated she felt from God during all her years of service. Many people were shocked by this. How could someone who seemed to be so deeply religious and obedient to God say such things?

The only way I can answer that is to ask if you've ever been desperately in love with someone. Your world revolves around this person and you want your beloved to respond to you in a certain way, but this person never does. Now, this person could love you just as much as you love in return, but because he or she never responds to you in the way you expect, you feel isolated, alone, vacant. Loneliness wraps its dark wings around you and you feel as if you're going to die. This can happen between lovers, husbands and wives, parents and children.

This can happen between you and God.

Many people say you shouldn't have expectations in your spiritual life. I don't believe this. Moses had expectations, so did Jonah, so did Paul, so did Christ. We should expect God to answer us, but we have to acquiesce to *the way* he responds.

He will respond, but watch out what you wish for, because once you get him started you can't shut him up.

For those times when spiritual dryness tempts you to give up, Richard Foster offers these words of comfort: "You must not be discouraged...There is a progression in the spiritual life, and it is wise to have some experience with lesser peaks before trying to tackle the Mt. Everest of the soul. So be patient with yourself.... You will be going against the tide, but take heart; your task is of immense worth" (*Celebration of Discipline*).

And to quote the Gospel of Matthew:

Ask and it will be given to you; seek and you will find; knock and the door will be opened to you. For everyone who asks receives; he who seeks finds; and to him who knocks, the door will be opened.

Which of you, if his son asks for bread, will give him a stone? Or if he asks for a fish, will give him a snake? If you, then ... know how to give good gifts to your children, how much more will your Father in heaven give good gifts to those who ask him! So in everything, do to others what you would have them do to you, for this sums up the Law and the Prophets. *(Matthew 7:7–15)*

Let's begin.

Chapter 6

BREATH PRAYER

A LL LIFE begins with a single breath, and so we begin these spiritual exercises by focusing on our breathing. Why? Besides the fact that deep, controlled, focused breathing is beneficial to our physical health, it also helps us shift our attention from whatever is on our minds—our problems, our desires, our responsibilities—to the gift we received from God at birth—breath.

The following simple exercise is a form of preprayer or premeditation. It's a way of clearing your mind and directing your concentration to God, and it's preparation for the first exercise we'll discuss, the Jesus Prayer.

- Find a comfortable place that's relatively quiet. Sit up straight or lie down and just relax for a few moments. Take a deep breath in and a deep breath out. Focus on your breath going in and out and repeat these words:
- Breathe in: "I am breathing in God."
- Breathe out: "God is breathing through me."

- Breathe in: "I am breathing in Christ."
- Breathe out: "Christ is breathing through me."
- Breathe in: "I am breathing in the Holy Spirit."
- Breathe out: "I am breathing out the Holy Spirit."
- Repeat until you feel your body and mind start to relax.

You can use your breath as a tool for any prayer or meditation that you perform. One way of using breathing is in the reciting of the Our Father. This allows us to focus on the words more clearly and will be used later on in this book when we talk about Centering Prayer and Lectio Divina. This is a simple rhythm you can perform.

- Breathe in and say: "Our Father,"
- Breathe out and say: "who art in heaven,"
- Breathe in and say: "hallowed be thy name."
- Breathe out and say: "Thy Kingdom come,"
- Breathe in and say: "thy will be done,"
- Breathe out and say: "on earth"
- Breathe in and say: "as it is in heaven."
- Breathe out and say: "Give us this day"
- Breathe in and say: "our daily bread,"
- Breathe out and say: "and forgive us our trespasses,"
- Breathe in and say: "as we forgive those"
- Breathe out and say: "that trespass against us."
- Breathe in and say: "And lead us not into temptation"
- Breathe out and say: "But deliver us from evil."
- Breathe in and say: "Amen."

Breath Prayer Exercise #1:
The Jesus Prayer

The Jesus Prayer originated among the Desert Fathers, a group of Christian holy men who lived in the arid regions of Egypt sometime around the fifth century. It is a simple meditative prayer and one that has been popularized by the classic nineteenth-century spiritual text known as *The Way of a Pilgrim*. That book, written by an anonymous Russian author, chronicles a simple peasant's search for God and how saying this prayer helped him to see God in all things.

My introduction to the prayer, however, didn't come from that book, but rather from *Franny and Zooey,* a novel by J. D. Salinger, the beloved author of *The Catcher in the Rye*. In this book, Franny and Zooey are sister and brother and the book is essentially two long discussions about the meaning of life. Franny, who is having a difficult time with her boyfriend, has picked up a copy of *The Way of the Pilgrim* and begins saying the Jesus Prayer to herself: "Lord Jesus Christ, have mercy on me." She repeats this prayer until she enters a certain trancelike state.

You can do that, I told myself when I had finished reading. Salinger's novel led me to *The Way of the Pilgrim,* which set me off on a journey of the Spirit I never thought possible.

But what exactly is this prayer? The author of *The Way of the Pilgrim* describes it this way:

> The Jesus Prayer is a continuous, uninterrupted call on the holy name of Jesus Christ with the lips, mind, and heart; and in the awareness of His abiding presence it is a plea for his undertakings, in all places, at all times, even in

sleep.... Anyone who becomes accustomed to this prayer will experience great comfort as well as the need to say it continuously. He will become accustomed to it in such a degree that he will not be able to do without it and eventually the Prayer will of itself flow in him.

At the heart of the prayer is repetition. You don't say the Jesus Prayer just once, you say it a hundred times, a thousand times, ten thousand times. You can say it before you go to sleep, in the moments after you wake up, when you're waiting at a traffic light, or standing on line at a grocery store. The prayer is made up of two parts. The first is an acknowledgment: *Lord Jesus Christ.* The second is a simple petition: *Have mercy on me.*

- Breathe in to the count of four.
- Hold for a count of four.
- Breathe out for a count of four.
- Hold for a count of four.
- Do this four times.
- On the fifth time, begin your prayer and follow this breathing pattern:
- Breathe in and repeat: "Lord Jesus Christ."
- Hold.
- Breathe out and repeat: "Have mercy on me."
- Hold.
- Repeat.

Breath Prayer Exercise #2:
Sacred Heart of Jesus

This prayer uses the form of the Jesus Prayer but substitutes a different image, that of the burning heart of Christ. Here we picture the enthusiastic, glowing heart of Christ, filled with the healing power of the Holy Spirit emanating from his chest. This is a prayer for increasing faith and to aid in healing.

Imagine the Holy Spirit flowing through the prism of Christ's divine heart. The light of divine love shines on you and brings you increased peace and warmth. It's important to focus on the image, to feel the warming effects of the Spirit and Christ touching you, enveloping you, increasing your awareness that you are one with God.

This prayer follows the same rhythm as the Jesus Prayer.

- Breathe in to the count of four.
- Hold for a count of four.
- Breathe out for a count of four.
- Hold for a count of four.
- Do this four times.
- On the fifth time, begin your prayer and follow this breathing pattern:
- Breathe in and repeat: "Sacred heart of Jesus."
- Hold.
- Breathe out and repeat: "I trust in you."
- Hold and repeat.

Breath Prayer Exercise #3:
Come, Holy Spirit, Come

This prayer is a petition for increased awareness of the Holy Spirit in your life. The Spirit is ever present, flowing through each and every one of us, tying together all of creation. Yet, we forget or don't realize the sometimes subtle flow of this divine person who exists and flows like energy from God the Father, through Christ, and into all of us.

This prayer is not a petition for the Holy Spirit to make an appearance in our lives, but to bring us to a level of awareness in which we realize that the Holy Spirit, the gift from God to all of us after the resurrection, is always present inside of us. We just need to let him out.

- Breathe in to the count of four.
- Hold for a count of four.
- Breathe out for a count of four.
- Hold for a count of four.
- Do this four times.
- On the fifth time, begin your prayer and follow this breathing pattern:
- Breathe in and repeat: "Come, Holy Spirit, come."
- Hold.
- Breathe out and repeat: "Come, Holy Spirit, come."
- Hold.
- Repeat.

Breath Prayer Exercise #4:
Only Say the Word and I Shall Be Healed

These words, a paraphrase of the words spoken by the centurion to Christ in Matthew's Gospel and intoned during the Catholic Mass, are a great way of asking God to bring spiritual, mental, physical, and emotional healing into your life.

- Breathe in to the count of four.
- Hold for a count of four.
- Breathe out for a count of four.
- Hold for a count of four.
- Do this four times.
- On the fifth time, begin your prayer and follow this breathing pattern:
- Breathe in and repeat: "Only say the word and I shall be healed."
- Hold.
- Breathe out and repeat: "Only say the word and I shall be healed."
- Hold.
- Repeat.

Chapter 7

CENTERING PRAYER

CENTERING PRAYER, like the Jesus Prayer, dates back to the time of the Desert Fathers and is a core teaching in *The Cloud of Unknowing*, a guide on how to pray, written by an anonymous English monk sometime during the fourteenth century. This monk wrote: "This is what you are to do: lift your heart up to the Lord with a gentle stirring of love, desiring him for his own sake and not his gifts. Center all your attention and desire on him and let this be the sole concern of your mind and heart."

It is a form of prayer that gained popularity in the twentieth century due in part to Trappist monks, including M. Basil Pennington, who describes it in his book *Centering Prayer* as "a simple method—a technique, if you like that term—to get in touch with what *is*."

In this prayer, through the grace of the God we focus our attention on the Holy Spirit, who lives within each and every one of us. How do we do this? By attempting to evacuate all the extraneous thoughts in our hearts and focus on a single representative word for that indwelling, for example, *God, Jesus, Spirit, love, faith,* or *strength.* It is a quiet form of prayer, one we do individually and in solitude.

Solitude, though, can be found in the strangest of places.

Between the hours of 4:00 and 7:00 PM on any given weekday, the streets around Pennsylvania Station in New York City are crowded with tens of thousands of weary—and during the summertime, sweaty—people with one goal in mind: to get the heck out of the city and go home. It was on one of those ordinary commuter days in the middle of a hot summer, standing in a swarm of people waiting for the traffic light to change at the intersection of 34th and 7th, that I happened to glance at the sandaled foot of a young woman who had the word *love* tattooed on her big toe.

Her big toe?

What in this young woman's mind compelled her to do such a thing? I'm not against tattoos, but that had to hurt! Why the

word *love* on her foot? As I imagined what it must have felt like to be stabbed innumerous times by a tiny needle, I was swept up in a frenzy of anxious commuters ready to trample me to paralysis if I didn't cross the street.

The tattooed woman also walked off and quickly disappeared into the crowd. As I descended into the mouth of Penn Station, I couldn't get the image of the love tattoo out of my mind. Soon thereafter a strange thing started to happen. Even though I was caught in the rush of the late afternoon commute, the world around me started slowing down and I began noticing tattoos everywhere.

There were Celtic designs, stars, Our Lady of Guadalupe, a birdcage, Elvis, a flag, a fish, a snake, and single words on different body parts on various people: *Mom, hope, faith, justice.* It seemed that just about every person in New York that day, from young teenagers to grandparents, was walking around with a tattoo.

What was going on here? Why had so many people decided to paint their bodies? Was it just a trendy thing to do? Or was there something else going on?

We live in a transient world. People are born. People age. People die. Some lose their hair. Some get fat—then skinny and fat again. We learn something new and then we forget it. We lose things, we find others. Houses are built. Apartments are torn down. Some days you have faith, some days you don't.

Other days you don't even want to hear the word *God* mentioned. The toy you loved so much as a child is thrown out by a parent. The job you dedicated so much of your life to is eliminated and you have to start all over again at the age of fifty. The girl you loved so much as a teenager breaks your heart, runs off with the drummer in your best friend's band, traipses off to France, returns with a new haircut, an earring in her nose, and a designer bag and moves to Minneapolis to become a TV weatherperson because she loved *The Mary Tyler Moore Show* and always wanted to stand in the middle of a busy street and throw her beret in the air. There is war and peace, love and hate, sadness and happiness, and don't even get me started on the mercurial experiences of bipolar disorder.

In our ever-changing world there is a desire for permanence. Your dog may leave you one day, but a tattoo, well, that's forever. The surge in tattooing, while maybe just the cool thing of the moment, seems to be indicative of a yearning to live in the presence of something everlasting, and it's this longing to understand with the heart the eternal, which is the core of Centering Prayer.

The girl with the toe tattoo was my first encounter with this type of devotion even though I didn't know it at the time. In Centering Prayer, you choose one word with sacred significance—*peace, faith, joy, Spirit, God, Christ*—and focus your attention on that particular word, repeating it to yourself until, through the grace of God, you begin to experience an internal shift. On that day, my word was *love*.

As I sat down on the always crowded 5:36 PM eastbounder to Long Island, snug between a sweaty guy with a hairnet and a woman who texted her BFF every thirty seconds, I started focusing on love, repeating it to myself. As the train lurched out of the station, my mind started to wander a bit—I was focusing on love, but then other things would enter my mind: worries, work, family, stop signs, lightbulbs, the Yankees, and Pez dispensers. Then my mind shifted back to love.

Love. God. Love. Christ. Love. Mother Teresa. The word *love* graffitied on a wall in Queens, New York. The homeless woman I pass on the street every day on my way to work. *Love. Resurrection. Love. God. Love.* Soon I experienced a tiny movement of the heart and I fell into a steady rhythm, and everything around me started to fall away. I couldn't feel the heat of sweaty dude next to me and I no longer heard texting girl chewing her gum. All the noise in the train vanished and I was lulled into this state where love was the primary focus.

Centering Prayer Exercise:
Find the Word in Your Heart

- Find a comfortable place where you won't be disturbed.
- Perform the premeditation breathing technique to calm you, repeating the Our Father as you consciously breathe in God and breathe out fear and stress.
- Begin with a short prayer of your own choosing, asking God to guide you in your focus. Ask God to help you quiet your mind and resensitize your heart.
- Find the word that comes to your heart. If nothing comes, focus on the word *Love*.
- Breathe the word in.
- Breathe the word out.
- Stay still, repeating the word to yourself, focusing the word in your heart that grows stronger with each beat. Then let the word go and sit in its presence as you would an old friend.
- Let it rest in you.

Chapter 8

LECTIO DIVINA

L ECTIO DIVINA, a form of Centering Prayer, is Latin for *holy reading,* in this case, the holy reading of Scripture. It is, as Adele Ahlberg Calhoun writes, "a way of entering deeply into the text with a heart alert to a unique and personal word from God. Words and verses that catch our attention become invitations to be with God in prayer."

A few years ago, I was going through yet another rough patch in my relationship with God and we (God and I) decided that we would go on retreat to try and recharge my spiritual batteries. Obviously, God's batteries were fine. Mine needed a power plant and some heavy-duty jumper cables.

Looking back, I see it was akin to a married couple who, having grown tired of each other, decide to go to the Poconos for a weekend—maybe get back some of that romance they'd lost. Imagine one of them is driving the car, talking ceaselessly, while the other stares blankly out the window at mountains and rest stops, worrying about work, questioning his or her existence, resting in self-loathing, thinking of failure and defeat, hearing nothing except the sound teachers make in the Charlie Brown cartoons. That's what it felt like to me.

The retreat was, spiritually speaking, a disaster from the start. I wasn't into it. I tried. I went through the motions—we spent time alone, I spoke, God spoke; we went for walks; we sat in front of the fireplace; we read books (I was reading Paulo Coelho's *The Fifth Mountain* about Elijah; God, of course, was reading the newspaper, the world section); we ate together. It went nowhere. I was there physically—and I really was trying—but I just wasn't feeling an emotional connection.

I went through this whole scenario in my head where I dumped God in a public place so there wouldn't be too much of a scene. There would be tears. There would be anger. Ultimately it was the best thing to do. I pictured myself valiantly walking away and swore I would never turn back.

In the end, I chickened out and decided I would dump God via a letter.

I walked to my room, switched on the laptop I brought with me, and started to type "Dear God," when the screen started flashing and I realized I needed to charge the battery. I went to my suitcase and soon realized I had left the power cable at home. While I was searching, the screen went black. Ugh. I then decided I needed to be out of that room, so I picked up my Bible and went for a walk.

We were staying at St. Ignatius Retreat House in New York. The grounds are small but beautiful: tree-filled and green with a few benches, and that day there was a warm breeze blowing from the east. I plopped myself down and opened the Bible.

I started to read. Nothing. *I give up.* I put the Bible next to me on the bench and the wind surged. The pages started flapping and I started smiling. "Up to your old tricks again," I said out loud. "Okay, you want to play biblical roulette, let's see what you got, old man!"

The wind blew the pages to the left and then to the right and then to the left again and it all sounded like a gambler shuffling cards. When the wind died down, I looked over and the Bible had come to rest on the story of the talents.

"Okay, you have my attention," I said. With that I started to read.

The Parable of the Talents

Again, it will be like a man going on a journey, who called his servants and entrusted his property to them. To one he gave five talents of money, to another two talents, and to another one talent, each according to his ability. Then he went on his journey. The man who had received the five talents went at once and put his money to work and gained five more. So also, the one with the two talents gained two more. But the man who had received the one talent went off, dug a hole in the ground and hid his master's money.

After a long time the master of those servants returned and settled accounts with them. The man who had received the five talents brought the other five. "Master," he said, "you entrusted me with five talents. See, I have gained five more."

His master replied, "Well done, good and faithful servant! You have been faithful with a few things; I will put you in charge of many things. Come and share your master's happiness!"

The man with the two talents also came. "Master," he said, "you entrusted me with two talents; see, I have gained two more."

His master replied, "Well done, good and faithful servant! You have been faithful with a few things; I will put you in charge of many things. Come and share your master's happiness!"

Then the man who had received the one talent came. "Master," he said, "I knew that you are a hard man, harvesting where you have not sown and gathering where you have not scattered seed. So I was afraid and went out and hid your talent in the ground. See, here is what belongs to you."

His master replied, "You wicked, lazy servant! So you knew that I harvest where I have not sown and gather where I have not scattered seed? Well then, you should have put my money on deposit with the bankers, so that when I returned I would have received it back with interest.

"Take the talent from him and give it to the one who has the ten talents. For everyone who has will be given more, and he will have an abundance. Whoever does not have, even what he has will be taken from him. And throw that worthless servant outside, into the darkness, where there will be weeping and gnashing of teeth."

(Matthew 25:14–30)

The word *talent* stayed with me, putting its arm around my shoulder, and just sat there as I went through a range of emotions: fear, hope, shame, love. I then remembered the story of Elijah and the wind and the whisper:

The Lord said, "Go out and stand on the mountain in the presence of the Lord, for the Lord is about to pass by."

Then a great and powerful wind tore the mountains apart and shattered the rocks before the Lord, but the Lord was not in the wind. After the wind there was an earthquake, but the Lord was not in the earthquake. After the earthquake came a fire, but the Lord was not in the fire. And after the fire came a gentle whisper. When Elijah heard it, he pulled his cloak over his face and went out and stood at the mouth of the cave.

Then a voice said to him, "What are you doing here, Elijah?" *(1 Kings 19:11–13)*

As I sat there listening to the wind in the trees, I thought of the many talents I had been given in my life and the times I had hidden them away. Emotion welled up inside me and my heart responded to the question God asked Elijah. My answer was two-fold: to give thanks and to ask for forgiveness.

Lectio Divina Exercise:
Praying with Scripture

- Make sure you have a Bible or a sacred piece of writing to read.
- Breathe: As I've mentioned before, it is a good idea to begin any prayer and meditation by taking a few moments to center yourself and become conscious of your breathing. Find a patch of silence inside you and go there.
- Read the Scripture passage. Try to take your time as you read the text. Even people familiar with certain stories are frequently surprised by the words or phrases that stand out during different readings. If something takes hold of you, stay with it. Allow your mind to quiet further and allow your soul to explore those words that have meaning for you. What is it about those particular phrases that speak to you?
- Meditate. Pause again and let the words settle into you. Enter the scene and begin pondering. Gently reflect on what you've read, prayed, and experienced. Do you feel anxious? Do you feel afraid? Are you happy or sad? What does this scene mean to you? If you were there that day, what would you have done?
- While you are doing this, take time to relax your mind and try not to think of anything in particular. It's a hard thing to do, but give God time to respond. During this time you may become distracted or bored. Your mind may race around a million little things: bills, commitments, family members, your dog, the color you want

to paint your bathroom. Your back may hurt or your backside might get numb. This is normal and is all part of the process. Allow the experience to occur, acknowledge it either verbally or mentally, then shift your focus back to your prayer and meditation. Do this as often as necessary. The more you enter into this direct communication with God, the easier it will become, as Henri Nouwen wrote in *The Wounded Healer,* to "make visible what was hidden, make touchable what was unreachable."

- Pray. Speak to God about what you're experiencing. Be open to God's response to you.
- Drop all words and allow yourself to be with God in the picture or idea of the text. Continue to focus on your breathing.

Part III

ENCOUNTERING GOD EXERCISES

A man stood outside a church in the middle of a busy city and watched as passersby went about their daily business. Many were shuffling off to work, others were walking around in shorts with newspapers and brown paper bags, still others seemed lost and in need of directions. Around noon, the man looked up at the tall steeple and fixed his gaze upon the thin iron cross that sat on the top. Every once in a while a man on his way to lunch or a woman on her way to the drugstore for cotton balls would slow down and look up, too. If the person lingered for a moment, the man would ask, "What is the Holy Spirit?" Many people said nothing and took his words as their cue to move on. Some said, "I don't know." Others said words like *God, Jesus, grass, smoke, fire, energy, a new line of sports shoes.* This went on for hours.

As the sun began to set, casting the street in the colors of Sri Lankan silk, and after hours of staring upward, his neck stiff and pinched, the man turned his gaze to the street. Walking toward him was a beautiful woman in a sundress. With the sun shining on her she looked as if she was radiating phosphorus.

"What is the Holy Spirit?" the man asked.

The beautiful woman smiled, looking like an angel from God. She raised her hand, her fingers painted in Technicolor, and slapped his face with the strength of a small Balkan army.

"That's the Holy Spirit," she said and walked away.

The man, his cheek burning with the fire of God, knew exactly what she meant.

Chapter 9

THE HOLY PRESSURE

WHAT THE WORLD is missing now is not a new religion or, for that matter, as many would argue, a new atheism. It's not missing a new brilliant technology for whitening teeth. It's most certainly not missing another cable TV station. Though poverty, lack of food, AIDS, war, and diminishing energy sources are all major concerns in the twenty-first century, and solutions to these crises are needed urgently, something else is missing from our world. Something that is so important that if you were to have it you could change your life right now. Not only that, *you could change the world.*

This thing is in short supply even though it's present among us right now. You can see the effects of this shortage in the eyes of many people you see every day—from the checkout clerk at a Walmart in Tennessee to the stock broker on Wall Street in New York City.

You know what we're critically missing now, more than anything else in the world?

Enthusiasm.

That inflammation of the soul, that fire in our hearts, that passion that drives us to new and glorious heights.

Many would disagree with me and argue that enthusiasm is all around us. Certainly, if you've ever been to a football game or a rock concert, you haven't just seen or heard enthusiasm—you've *experienced* its power. What about wedding parties? Well, yes, those are some excited people at these gatherings, especially the drunk ones (people to this day still talk about my wedding). What about the stock market and all those people in the pit, flailing their arms and buying or selling? All those people are enthusiastic, right?

And what about all those *bad* people? It's certainly true that we live in a time in history when religious fanaticism is a very big concern. Enthusiasm can be about being passionate for a cause, and while this might sound like a political or ideological statement, I assure you it is not. I am not advocating zealotry or fanaticism, both of which abuse enthusiasm's essence and exploit it the way pornography exploits sex.

What some people take for enthusiasm is little more than just misdirected energy—the way, the night before a test, a normally studious schoolboy jacks himself up on soda and chocolate and spends his time bouncing off the walls instead of putting his nose in a book. What you have the next day is a tired, dehydrated young man staring at an almost blank page in class, mentally kicking himself in the rear for not having spent time doing what he should have done the night before—studying. The boy was certainly filled with energy but none of us would argue that he was being enthusiastic.

Then what do I mean by *enthusiasm*? Let's look for a moment at the definition of the word. According to *Merriam-Webster's Collegiate Dictionary,* enthusiasm comes from the Greek word *enthousiasmos,* to be inspired from God (*en-theos*) and means to have "a belief in the special revelations of the Holy Spirit."

What the world is missing now isn't misdirected energy, it is an outpouring—a flowing awareness—of the living presence of the Holy Spirit that exists in each and every one of us.

Imagine for a moment nothing except your kitchen sink. If you don't have a kitchen sink, that's okay, imagine your bathroom sink. Imagine that your sink has a single handle and you can turn it on and off rather easily. Behind the wall is a series of interconnected, high-pressure pipes that bring the water from a larger source, a reservoir or a water tower or a local water station into your home. When the water is shut off on your sink, a tiny valve closes that prevents water from flowing. When that valve is closed, the water behind it is under pressure. Extreme pressure. It's sitting there in that pipe and wants badly to be unleashed. Yet, you control when the water is turned on and you also determine how powerful the flow is.

The water is always there. The potential is always just a few centimeters behind a tiny, yet powerful valve.

You may lift the handle only slightly to get a trickle of water as you wet your toothbrush. You may lift the valve all the way to get a powerful steady stream of water in order to wash your dishes.

Imagine that water is the Holy Spirit, and imagine there is a faucet connected to your heart. Focus on the heart and focus on this faucet, which is connected to a pipe that contains the Holy Spirit. The Spirit is under intense pressure. He's pushing on the valve of your faucet heart. You can feel that pressure when you wake up in the morning, throughout your day at work, when you are stuck in traffic, in the moments before sleep.

It's the holy pressure.

Keep this image in your mind. Turn on the faucet.

The Holy Spirit Exercise

How is the Spirit flowing through you? Or is he flowing through you? Is the valve open or closed in your heart? Are you living a life where you have turned the valve open all the way to let the Spirit flow strongly and steadily through your life? Or are you living each day drip by drip by drip?

However you answered that question, I want you to reach inside your heart and increase the flow by lifting the handle of the faucet. If the valve was totally shut off and nothing was getting through, I want you to imagine opening the faucet slightly and pray this simple prayer: "Flow through me, Holy Spirit. Flow through me."

If the Spirit has been dripping through you, I want you to increase the stream in your life. Repeat: "Flow through me, Spirit. Flow through me."

Repeat one thousand times daily.

Chapter 10

HEROES AND ARKS

MY FIVE-YEAR-OLD SON wants to be a superhero. Not just one superhero, but many: Spider-Man, Superman, Batman, Green Lantern, a Power Ranger, and most recently Luigi, the plumber/superhero brother of Mario from the Super Mario Bros. video games. He'll dress up like these characters and act out different scenarios. Sometimes he's saving a princess or knocking out a bad guy (usually me—I'm the villain most of the time). He wants to save the world.

I love superheroes, too, and I wanted to introduce him to one of my favorites, Indiana Jones—the archeologist/adventurer from those great action-packed movies by Steven Spielberg and George Lucas. After a long dinnertime debate with my wife about some of the content, I threw the movie *Raiders of the Lost Ark* into the DVD player, sat my son down, and said, "Okay, you have to watch this."

He was riveted.

So was I. Not just for the awesome action sequences, but because this movie took on a whole new meaning in my life.

Do you know the story of *Raiders of the Lost Ark*? Our hero Indiana Jones is asked to track down the famed and legendary ark of the covenant before the Nazis, in the years before World War II, locate it to use for devious purposes. Now, the ark is this box that holds the Ten Commandments, the stone tablets that God gave to Moses and that the ancient Hebrews treasured and carried with them wherever they went. At some point in history the ark went missing. It has been sought after ever since, because it is said that whoever wields the ark will have great power—the power of God.

As I was watching the movie, my mind started to race.

The Ten Commandments were God's covenant with the Israelites, an agreement between the Lord and his people. "Follow my commandments and you follow me and you will be called blessed." These were the Word of God and there was great power in those words.

That agreement lasted for thousands of years, but then along came this guy Christ. Christ became the new covenant, not just with one group of people, but a covenant for all people. Only Christ didn't live long; he died a relatively young man. Yet, before he died he promised to leave behind an advocate, a Paraclete, an advisor who would be the living presence of God in all our lives. That protector was and is the Holy Spirit.

After Christ's death, resurrection, and ascension, the Holy Spirit makes his presence known to the apostles and in turn becomes a living fire that burns in each and every one of us. This means that each of us carries within the Word of God, the new agreement, the new covenant. This in turn means that each of us is an ark of the covenant. Each of us is a container for the great and awesome power of God. This does not make us God, but

God is present in every one of us. Every one of us contains the awesome power of God.

"Now," you might be saying, "don't talk about such things. God doesn't want us to be powerful, he want us to be humble. Humility is nothing more than knowing your place."

You and I are not God, we are human beings with God living in us. Yet too often humility becomes confused with low self-esteem. Over our lifetimes, many of us have come to believe that in order to show humility to God we need to think of ourselves as lowly, sinful, base creatures. Blame religion. Blame society. Blame philosophers. Blame our families.

This is not what God wants for us. Certainly, God wants us to be aware of our sinfulness, but God calls us to be heroes, to be strong, to help save ourselves, and in turn to save the lives of others.

Christ redefines for us what it means to be truly human. For thousands of years we lived as children of Adam, the fallen man. Christ, through the miracle of his resurrection, calls us to live a new life and in the process to engage in a constant redefinition of what it means to be human. Christ is our model for this new interpretation. Christ is the hero to be emulated.

What is a hero? A hero is a person who takes action to help people. That is what the Holy Spirit calls us to do. When the Spirit descended on Mary after the angel Gabriel told her she was to be the mother of Jesus, what did she do? She took action. She packed her things and journeyed to her cousin Elizabeth. To do what? To serve her. When the Holy Spirit descended on Christ after his baptism by John, what did he do? He took action and did what? He began his ministry and began serving. When the Spirit descended on the apostles at Pentecost, what did they do?

They relinquished fear and began serving the people. Not just one group of people but all people, of all nations.

We, too, are called to serve, to not be afraid. With the Holy Spirit already in us, there is no time to waste. We need to take action now and assist those around us, whether it's a family member, a friend, a coworker, a stranger on the street, our environment, our nation, or our world.

How Can I Serve? Exercise

Each morning, as part of your prayer, ask God this very important question: "How can I serve?" Then be quiet and allow God to answer. You may not get an answer right away, but keep asking that question. Allow these words "How can I serve?" to become for you like the Jesus Prayer, words spoken to yourself during the day and through the night. Let the words become your breath.

Chapter 11

FEEL IT, SEE IT, TASTE IT, HEAR IT, SMELL IT

I F YOU'RE A CHRISTIAN and have attended church for a number of years, you've probably heard the following, oh, maybe a million times: "God loved us so much that he sent his only son to us so he could save us from our sins."

Well, that's just great. They are important words for Christians. Very important. They formulate a basic tenet of our faith. Yet what do those words really mean to you and to me? Even though we have images here, "God," "love," "son," "sins," the thought is an abstraction. These words live somewhere in our minds. They are just words.

Conversion, a movement toward God, happens when the words become flesh to us. Christ is, as John's Gospel says, the Word. Yet he is just a concept until he becomes flesh, becomes man. When God takes on the role of divine human in our history, that is when stuff gets good. The words need to become flesh. They need to be touched. We need to feel them and to have our hearts breathe life into them.

Too much of our faith is caught up in abstraction, and these abstractions end up becoming theological clichés. "Christ died for our sins." "God loves you." Yes, this is great, thank you, but what does this mean to us as human beings?

One of the problems with the human condition—and this is why genocides happen—is that unless something is happening to us directly, it's very hard to feel sympathy or compassion. This is not to say that there aren't sympathetic or compassionate people in the world. But if I have a headache, no matter how painful a headache it is, you cannot experience that headache for me. That is my own personal pain. It does not involve you unless I become angry or rude or ask you for an aspirin. Then it affects you.

In order for us to be compassionate, we need, even if it's only momentarily, to imagine we are suffering the pain. Usually people who have suffered are the most compassionate because they know what it's like. This is the Jesus problem and why so many of us have a hard time with our faith. We cannot *feel* all this love that our religion tells us we should be feeling.

One way of transcending this predicament is to engage the imagination, to move beyond words and into images. One of the easiest ways of doing this is to select a favorite piece of Scripture, read it a few times to familiarize yourself with the basic story, and then use your imagination to visualize yourself as deeply in the scene as humanly possible. You can imagine that you are either the main character—maybe Jesus or Mary—or a bystander watching from the sidelines. Then you engage your senses.

Imagination Exercise

Suppose you pick the scene in Exodus where God reveals himself to Moses through a burning bush. Open your heart and use your senses: look, listen, feel, smell, taste the scene and make it as real as you can. Imagine Mount Sinai and the vistas Moses sees when he looks out across the land. Imagine what Moses looks like. What is he wearing? Are his sandals worn? Is he hungry? Is he tired? Disillusioned? Faithful? Excited? Imagine the wind blowing through his hair, but not only imagine it, *feel it*. Remember a time in your life when you felt wind on your face and bring that to your meditation. Try to feel what Moses might have felt on top of that mountain, with very little water, alone.

Then imagine the bush. It can be as big or small as you want it. Imagine it starting to burn—slowly, smoldering at first. The smoke fills Moses' nostrils. It fills your nostrils as well. He watches it burn. You watch it burn. He's perplexed at what he is seeing. Even though wildfires are common in this arid region of the world, this bush doesn't seem to be burning into ashes.

Imagine what you would have felt if you were in the desert valley of a mountain. Imagine what you would have felt if the bush started talking to you. How is the bush communicating to you? Through words? Through impressions? Through inspired feelings? Is there an inner voice talking to you, or are you hearing the thunderous boom of the Almighty? What does the bush say? How would you react?

Take the time to quiet your mind and listen. You may not hear anything. Your mind may again race to something you need to take care of at work or at home. Accept it and then let it go and listen to the scene you are in. What do you hear?

Chapter 12

THE RESURRECTION: PAST, PRESENT, FUTURE

IMAGINE FOR A MOMENT a huge, flat-roofed, glass house. It has three floors. On the bottom floor is your past—all the things that have ever happened to you. The second floor is your present, only it's not as crowded as the first floor because your present moment is really fleeting. In some ways, your present is like the middle part of a child's slide in a park. Your future lingers at the top for a moment and then takes off. That middle part of the slide, when you're sliding, that's the present. Before you know it, you land on the bottom and your feet touch the ground in your past.

The present moment is so hard to hold on to, isn't it? I mean, let's try to hold on to the present moment coming up.

Ready.

Set.

Go.

Grab it!

Did you catch it?

Me neither.

So, we have the first two floors. The third floor is your future—all the events in your life that haven't happened yet. The future is constantly changing depending on how you slide through your present moment. Maybe as you're sliding down, you put your feet out and slow down your momentum, or maybe you look to the side and see a friend and wave. Maybe you hiccup. Every little change on the way down affects when the future takes flight.

So, to sum up so far: we have a glass house and it contains all of your experiences. Your past. Your present. Your future.

The Glass House Exercise #1:
The Glass Elevator

Let's pretend there's a glass elevator connected to the top of the house and you can ride this elevator up high into the sky. The elevator has a glass floor so you can see down clearly as you lift off.

As you ascend, look down at your life now.

What do you see?

Let's call this God's, or the universe's, viewpoint. Your past, present, and future appear as if they are happening simultaneously. There is no sense of time because from this point of view, it's all happening at once. This means that eternity isn't something linear, starting six billion years ago and continuing on six billion years into the future and beyond. Eternity isn't big at all. It's a single point, a still point, as T. S. Eliot said, in space. The farther you fly into the sky, the more difficult it becomes to see any separation in time, to see any separation of bodies or space. Climb even higher and you see that bodies occupy the same space. Eternity isn't something vast. It's a single, glorious, beautiful moment.

Imagine that this is happening for all people. That the glass house itself is vast and there are people who intersect your life at certain spaces. Maybe someone intersects with you in your future, but because time is just a single moment, when you meet that person in the present, it's as if you knew him always. Or maybe a person runs into you in your past and the two of you talked over a cup of coffee that you don't remember because it happened in his past and you're pretty involved with your present. Then this person appears again in your future—which is really just your present when it finally happens—and there's a familiarity that's uncanny. Maybe you kissed this person at a space in your life. Or maybe you shook this person's hand or bummed a cigarette off that person somewhere in your past—or future—and when you met each other in the present it was as if you always knew that person.

So a man, separated from his beloved by geography for months, is actually spending time with her right now. And a Monday night in a bar in August so long ago, when he was gently overwhelmed by how pretty her hand looked and how her arm, long and distant like a horizon, freckled with stars, made him lose his breath, wasn't a single occurrence but a constant happening that continues to unfold right now.

What am I trying to say? That our lives have intersected many times in this single moment in eternity. Which in turn means that Christ's life, death, and resurrection weren't single occurrences that happened two thousand years ago but are events happening in our lives right now, right here, right in front of you even though you may not be aware of it. Whether we know it or not, we are participating in a single eternal moment.

God, Christ, the Holy Spirit are present here. Among and within. Everything you do affects not just the people in your immediate life, but the lives of all people, whether it's a neighbor you've never spoken to or an old man with sweaty hands in Beijing.

The Glass Elevator Exercise #2:
Shared Space

Imagine for a moment that there are two people standing about ten feet from one another, their feet somehow locked to the ground. Oh, and that they are standing beneath a glass elevator. Let's imagine that these two people are mortal enemies. They are each other's archnemesis. Maybe they're snarling at each other or saying a few choice words, but they are not allowed to move and for this exercise they won't. You, however, will.

Where are you? Well, you're inside the glass elevator and it's crystal clear (before you got in, someone really scrubbed that thing down with vinegar and newspaper). You look down and you see these two below you.

You press the button, the motor engages, and you move upward, let's say one story. You look down. The enemies are still there. Still about ten feet away from each other. You press the button again and ascend about four more stories. You look down. There they are, exchanging hand gestures, but something seems a bit different. You can't tell what, but something seems strange.

You move up another fifty feet. You are now one hundred feet above the two enemies and it dawns on you what's happening. From this height, it seems that the two enemies are much closer together than when you first saw them.

You rise another nine hundred feet. You are now a thousand feet above them. You know they cannot move, but now with your excellent vision it seems the distance between them has been cut in half. You rise higher, doubling your distance, and now it seems that the two people below you are only inches away from each other. You rise higher, miles over the two people, and they look as if they are maybe an inch away from each other. You burst through the atmosphere as you rise higher into space and the two enemies appear to be sharing the same space.

You continue moving into space and soon towns and countries all dissolve into a single cell, or a pale blue dot, as Carl Sagan once said.

This is how God sees us: not as separate. Not as distant from one another, but as members of the body of Christ. You share the same space with a billion other people. What you do to your neighbor, you do to yourself, what you do to the lesser, Christ says, you do to me.

Imagine someone you don't like. Someone you detest. Someone you need to forgive. Imagine you are standing across from that person beneath the glass elevator, which is equipped with a camera that projects your image and the image of your enemy onto a large TV screen. As the empty elevator rises, leaving the two of you earthbound, you watch on the screen as the distance between you narrows until you occupy the same piece of land.

Chapter 13

THE HANDS OF GOD

I N   O U R   F A S T - P A C E D, hectic world it is sometimes very easy to let our worries burden us and take control of our lives. When life's problems have become too big, when we've done all we can do and can do no more, it's time to turn them over to a higher power and place them in the hands of God.

The hand of God is a universal symbol, one depicted in art and words over the centuries. From the 37th Psalm, "If the LORD delights in a man's way, he makes his steps firm; though he stumble, he will not fall, for the LORD upholds him with his hand," to Auguste Rodin's sculpture *The Hand of God,* which depicts the creation of man, to the words of Norman Vincent Peale: "Put yourself in God's hands. To do that simply state, 'I am in God's hands.' Then believe you are NOW receiving all the power you need. 'Feel' it flowing into you" (*The Power of Positive Thinking*).

In this meditation you will place your problems in the hands of God.

God's Hands Exercise

Imagine before you two outstretched hands. The palms are up and the hands come together as if they are cupping water. Hold that image in your mind until it becomes very clear. You can picture the valley these two hands create and you can see the lines of the palms that look like the contours of a map. These are big hands. These are strong hands. These are powerful hands.

Consider another image. With your eyes still closed, think of a problem in your life, something you've been worrying about but over which you have absolutely no control. Maybe you have a toothache and you've called your dentist and she can't see you until tomorrow afternoon because she's lounging on a beach in Mexico. Maybe you're late on your rent because an important check hasn't cleared for you. Maybe your husband or wife is having a difficult time at work and the horror of layoffs hangs over your heads. Maybe a dear friend of yours is sick. Whatever it is, picture the problem in your mind. Okay. Got it?

I want you to take that image, that problem, the thing you've been worrying about and I want you to place it in the open hands we talked about earlier. How do you do that? You can imagine the problem as if it's a snapshot, a photograph, or a still life and imagine yourself laying the problem in the palms of these two humongous hands.

Repeat these words: "I place my problems in the hands of God and have faith that everything will work out the way it is supposed to."

Chapter 14

THE EXAMEN

A FEW YEARS AGO I became a father. My wife and I came to a very important decision after we brought our son home from the hospital. It had nothing to do with his diet or religion or what school he would eventually would attend. It had to do with video games.

My wife and I agreed that we would keep our son away from video games for as long as possible. Both of us had spent years in front of a TV playing the likes of Super Mario Bros. and Donkey Kong and dozens of others. We did not want our children to waste as much time as we did (and we each spent a serious amount of time playing when we could have been spending time with our respective families or friends or reading or praying or doing whatever).

We were very good with our first child. Granted, some people thought we were raising him in the Amish tradition because he didn't know what a game controller was, but we were good for four years.

And then...

Enter our son's Aunt Josie.

Josie loves video games.

When my wife was in the hospital delivering our second child, our four-year-old son spent the night with his aunt, who introduced him to Nintendo.

It was over.

All the hard work. All the talking in secret codes for four years was ruined by my sister-in-law.

Over the next few months all I heard was a crying baby and our son whining for me to buy him a Nintendo DS, a handheld computer game. I refused! No son of mine was going to waste all his time playing video games. (I did feel a bit like Saint Augustine who, after fathering a child and living a lascivious life, converted to Christianity and then said no one could ever do what he did because it was naughty.)

Well, my son kept asking. He kept knocking. I caved.

I ordered my son a Nintendo from Amazon and three days later it arrived in the mail. The moment I saw that box, I knew I had done a bad thing, so I just left the box in the living room as I debated what to do. To give or not to give, that was the question. My son had no idea I had ordered the game for him and he kept nagging me to buy one for him.

Then something started to happen. I started looking at the box in a way I never expected. My son would pass that box every day and not once did he ever think to ask, "Hey, what's inside the box?" He would be inches away from it. Sometimes he would run his small hand over the lettering, but at no time did he ever suspect that what he desired, the thing he wanted most in life, was actually already in his presence.

Something took form in me and I felt it rise inside me. That box for me became God. I don't mean it changed shape or started talking to me, and I definitely don't mean it turned into a golden idol that I worshipped. But I saw God in that box.

So many of us have this desire, this yearning to know God, to be with God, to have joy in God, and many of us go on long, arduous journeys to find him. But how many of us ever ask, *Is God here with me now? Is the God I desire here with me right now? And if he is, how do I react to him?*

These questions form the basis of the examen.

The examen, a core component of Saint Ignatius's teaching, involves setting aside time to reflect on the activities and thoughts of the day. In this simple meditation, we ask ourselves primarily two questions: Where was God for me? What was my response to those encounters?

This examen is a gentle, and sometimes startling, way of finding God in our daily lives and helps us to learn from our actions—and reactions. Many of us may talk a good game; we may talk about love for God and neighbor or speak excitedly about the gifts in our lives, but our actions say otherwise. The examen is a bit like a spiritual chiropractor that helps to bring your desires in alignment with God's will—and conversely, it helps to bring your will in alignment with God's desire.

Oh, and did I give my son the Nintendo? Of course. I'm a pushover.

Examen Exercise

Many people suggest performing the examen twice a day, around lunchtime and then again before you go to sleep, but it can be done at any time of the day.

Step 1: Using one of the breathing techniques discussed earlier in this book, attempt to quiet your mind. You might resist, but don't put pressure on yourself to conform to any preconceived notion about what your silence should be. Just allow yourself to be.

Step 2: Remind yourself that God is all around you. He's inside you and outside you and his heart beats in all creation.

Step 3: Ask the Holy Spirit to rise up inside you and give you the wisdom to acknowledge God in your life and the gifts that are all around you. Ask the Spirit for guidance in reviewing your actions.

Step 4: Give thanks for the day. Turn your eyes into microscopes and look for God in all things, the good and the bad. Find God in a book you are reading, in music you're listening to, in your loved ones as well as in the rude bus driver who's always barking at you, the annoying coworker with the staring problem, and the electric bill that arrives in the mail. Finding God in a flower can be easy. Finding God in some jerk who cuts you off in traffic—well, there's the rub.

Step 5: Take inventory of your day. Ask questions and give honest answers.
- Where was God for you today?
- Was he walking with you or did you ignore him the way a child ignores a friend he's grown tired of?
- Was God present in your actions?
- Was he present in your thoughts?
- If God was giving you the silent treatment, was it God who was being difficult or were you wearing earplugs?
- Did you show love to people?
- Were you rude and treated a person unfairly?
- Did you really have to send that e-mail?
- Were you trying to get one over on a co-worker?
- Did you show the people in your life love?
- Did you show strangers love?

Step 6: With the help of the Holy Spirit, make it a priority to reconcile your actions. If you feel you failed, ask God for guidance, strength, and forgiveness. And if you did a good job, well, be excited and build on that gift.

Chapter 15

DYING TO GOD

I DIED ONE NIGHT, some years ago, on a fog-entrenched medieval bridge in an Eastern European city.

When I was in my mid-twenties, a few years out of college, I had this harebrained, Ralph Kramden–like scheme to change my life. I was going to live mythically. What exactly did I mean by that? I wanted to imitate the life of Christ. The first way I was going to do that was to spend forty days and forty nights in the desert. Now, I'm pretty fair-skinned and I burn rather easily in the sun—plus, the heat makes me feel really uncomfortable—so I decided to substitute the streets of Europe for the arid, sun-scorched sands of a barren wilderness. I would much prefer coffee and chocolate pastries than a diet of morning dew and locusts.

Seriously convinced that this was the right thing to do, and with very little money in my pocket (not to mention a bank account filled not with greenbacks but with cobwebs), I quit my job and set off to work out my salvation. (I was in my twenties at the time, so cut me some slack!)

In the middle of this journey I found myself standing on the blackened, cobblestoned walkway of the Charles Bridge, in Prague—a seven-hundred-year-old construction adorned with life-size statues of Jesus and the saints. I was with my friend Anna, who was living in the city at the time. It was a cool night in October. There was a full moon and a fog was circling around everything like a lazy, fat cat that wanted to go to sleep.

We were not alone. The bridge, a central artery that connected the Old Prague with the New Prague, was a magnet for tourists, street artists, lovers, and the lost. Many of us that night had formed a loose circle around two musicians—a guitarist and a violinist, who were playing a Rachmaninoff piece—when a well-dressed man in designer clothes, long brown hair, and a beard bisected the crowd and stood before us staring at the moon.

"Look," I said to my friend, "it's Jesus."

"Yes," she said. "Resurrection has been good to him."

We both smiled, and as I watched this man, who seemed entranced by the moon and the music and the night, something began to change inside me. I felt surprised and unsettled, as if I had been given a gift I wasn't expecting. Time seemed to perform a slow somersault, and a few words of a joke only a moment ago began to awe and frighten me. My eyes darted around the bridge. Chills seemed less to come from within me as much as to be pressed upon me.

I was looking at the face of Christ.

Not just this rich man in Gucci and Armani, but the musicians, the beggars, the lovers holding hands, the students, the children, all these strangers—all these people I would never see again—seemed to remove the mask of their temporal existence and beneath all these exposed faces was the visage of Christ. Then the words of Paul came flooding into my mind:

The body is a unit, though it is made up of many parts; and though all its parts are many, they form one body. So it is with Christ. For we were all baptized by one Spirit into one body—whether Jews or Greeks, slave or free—and we were all given the one Spirit to drink.

Now the body is not made up of one part but of many.... Now you are the body of Christ, and each one of you is a part of it. *(1 Corinthians 12:12–14, 27)*

I died that night and have never been the same again.

Anyone who sees God's face will die.

I remember these words from my early days in Catholic school: "Moses then said, 'Please show me your glory.' Yahweh said, 'I shall make all my goodness pass before you, and shall pronounce the name Yahweh.... But my face,' he said, 'you cannot see, for no human being can see me and survive'" (see Exod. 33:18–20).

Some teachers love to scare the God out of us, and those words certainly did the trick for me, so much so that I would pray at night never to see the face of God.

"Ask and it will be given to you." Well, I asked and God gave me what I wanted. Spiritual blindness.

For years I would just look at people as people. I never saw God in anything. God was distant. God was frightening. God was Medusa. Look upon him and you would turn to stone.

Yet, after that spiritual—and very real—death in Prague, I was resurrected in a profound and simple way. I had been transformed and began to see God in all things—not only in the people I passed in the street, my family, my friends, and even my enemies, but in the land I walked on, the buildings I stood beneath, the bread I ate, the wine I drank, even the plastic I threw away in a garbage can. Certainly if we are created in God's image then the face of my neighbor is the face of God. If Christ is God fully present in human form, then the face of a one-legged, toothless beggar staring back at me on a city street is the face of Christ asking for help.

We are, as Paul says in 1 Corinthians 6, the temple of the Holy Spirit. In turn each of us is an ark of the covenant, the chest that held the Ten Commandments, only this time we contain within us the Word of God, Christ, who is present in us through the power of the Holy Person, otherwise known as the Holy Spirit. To look at others and see God within them is a gift for us.

Yet, this gift is an uncomfortable one, one in fact that shames me, because more often than not I turn away from God's face. I don't want to die to my old ways. No matter how many people like to romanticize dying in poetry, literature, and theology, dying sucks. It's painful and frightening. Dying to God is no less than that.

Yet when I have allowed the Holy Spirit to flow courage through my soul and actually looked upon the face of God, it is the most beautiful of all experiences. In that death is the seed of resurrection—a new life—one where, if only for a moment, you remove your own mask and expose, if ever so briefly, the Christ within you that yearns to show his face to others.

Dying to God Exercise

Imagine for a moment that you are standing a hundred feet away from a painting of the face of Christ. It doesn't matter what that face looks like. It could be a famous work of art, an image from a movie, a child's crayon drawing—whatever makes you feel most comfortable. Now, recite the Jesus Prayer and take a step toward that image. Repeat the prayer and take a step. You're getting closer to the painting. What may have looked like something the size of stamp from that initial distance is starting to grow in size.

As you repeat the prayer, move closer to the painting. As you do, you begin to notice the painting isn't a painting at all. It's a mosaic, and the closer you get, the more you realize that this mosaic is made up of tiny images of people whose lives have intersected your own. There are photos of people in your family, friends, strangers, coworkers, people you don't remember but whom you passed in the streets or on the highway. There is the waitress from the diner you visited when you were ten and the teacher you had a crush on, whose name you've long forgotten.

As you move closer, the images become bigger and bigger and you begin to notice that the photos making up this mosaic are in fact also mosaics themselves, and within those are more images of people who have crossed their lives with yours. Continue moving closer to the image, repeating the Jesus Prayer, and keep your eyes and mind open for Christ. He's in there waiting for you to notice.

Chapter 16

THANKSGIVING

I T I S V E R Y E A S Y to take our world, our loved ones, ourselves, and our God for granted. Every morning when we wake up, throughout the day, and before we go to sleep we should take a few moments to give thanks. But *not too much thanks,* as the following story demonstrates.

The setting is an office in New York City. A confused, disorganized young man is trying to collate a number of different reports. Enter a level-headed young woman who gives the young man a paper clip. He looks at her and he looks at the clip. For a moment he's speechless. Smiling, he shuffles his papers around and slips on the clip. There is a sigh of relief and then the lights dim and a spotlight shines on the young man, who turns to a nonexistent audience and begins to speak.

"Oh my. Wow. I can't even believe this. This is such an honor. This paper clip changed my life and I just want to say thanks to a few people for making this happen.

"First off, I would like to thank my coworker Darya who gave me this paper clip. If it weren't for her kindness and generosity, I wouldn't be standing here today.

"I would like to thank Pete in the mail room. Pete is the guy who brings the supplies we order to our offices. He's always friendly, and Pete, I know you're working two jobs to support your family and I want to say thank you just for bringing Darya that box of paper clips. I want to thank your family, too, for the sacrifices they have to make because you work so much. They know you love them.

"I would like to thank the paper supply company that shipped those clips to our office. Thank you just for having a business that keeps us from losing our minds. Thank you not only to the heads of the company but to all your employees who are the backbone of the corporation.

"I would like to thank the UPS guy who makes deliveries to our office every day. I would also like to thank your parents, man, for bringing you into the world. Thank you.

"I would like to thank the manufacturers of the cardboard that created the box that holds the paper clips and all those workers in your plant who show up for work every day, in desperate need of caffeine, but ready to work. Thank you to all their families as well, including all sons and daughters who might be getting married and starting families of their own soon.

"A special shout-out to the people who make the ink that's printed on the cardboard box and the designer who designed the logo. You guys never get the credit you deserve. Keep on rocking.

"Thank you to the truck drivers who move the supplies from the warehouse to the stores, and thanks to all the civil engineers who helped design all the roads that we all drive on every day, and the municipal workers who keep the roads *relatively* clean and safe (I just ran over a pothole the other day). Oh, and thank you to those folks who create the traffic lights that prevent chaos in our nation.

"Thank you to all the people who fed and clothed all these people.

"I would also like to thank the inventors of the paper clip, including Samuel B. Fay, Erlman J. Wright, and all the folks at Britain's Gem Manufacturing Company who worked back in the 1890s to get clips out to the world. And a special thanks to Johan Vaaler of Norway. I know it's been proven that Johan is not the originator of the paper clip, but without him we wouldn't have all the folklore and legend surrounding this little bit of metal. And we definitely wouldn't have that giant paper clip sculpture outside the Norwegian School of Management in Sandvika, Norway.

"I know these paper clips are manufactured in China, which is wild, right? How many thousands of miles need to be traversed to get those clips from overseas? It's unfathomable to me. Anyway, I would like to thank all the folks in China who work in the factories that produce these clips as well as the drivers and all the dockworkers on both sides of the world who were involved in getting the clips from the factory to the ports.

"Thank you to all the people who mined the metal for these clips, and thank you to all the animals and plants that were displaced during this time so I could hold my paper together.

"And last, I want to thank God who has been involved in this project from its inception and was in all the people and things that helped along the way. We are all connected and we do live in abundance even if we sometimes feel disconnected and empty. Thank you, God. Thank you. Thank you. Thank you!"

This is why it's not good to be too thankful. If you were, you'd never get out of bed and you'd probably never get any work done. So use common sense when giving thanks, but make sure you do it every day.

The Acceptance Speech Exercise #1:
Did You See God Today?

When you wake up in the morning or right before you go to sleep, take a few moments to give thanks to God, the people, and the things in your life by tracing how each intersects with your existence. Of course people are more important than things, but each thing is infused with the life of the people who assisted in creating it. Each person, in turn, is infused with God the Creator.

Then ask this question: *Did I notice God in that person and thing today?* If the answer is no, ask yourself why and then ask the Holy Spirit for guidance in your search.

Chapter 17

THE GEOMETRY OF THE CROSS

PICTURE for a moment a simple cross. You can even draw one if that helps. It's easy. A cross, after all, is a very simple drawing. It is really just two lines that run over each other.

Now, I hate to do this to you, but I would like to talk briefly about math—geometry, to be more specific. I promise this will take only a few moments.

One of the most basic ideas in geometry is that when two lines intersect they do so at a single point. Let's look at the picture of the cross you drew, only this time I want you to think of the line moving from the bottom to the top as God, and then I want you to consider the line moving from left to right as Man.

You will see that these two lines meet at a specific point in space. Let's call that point *Christ*.

Here we have the line of eternity, the timeless, the infinite God, intersecting with the line of the time-bound, the temporal, the finite Man. Spirit crossing flesh, coming together at one point in time and space—Christ, the infinite man.

Let's consider that the line of God includes all his creation:

birds, mountains, rivers, shopping malls, barracks, your family, strangers, even rude people on cell phones or behind the wheels of an endless array of SUVs in grocery store parking lots. Let's also consider that the man in question is you.

Examining this new information, we will see that whenever or wherever we encounter God's creation, no matter how beautiful or how ugly, no matter how loving or how annoying, we intersect at one point and that point is Christ. Where we find God's creation—all his creation—we will also find Christ. No matter where you turn or what you do, he is there, in front of you, behind you, cooing at you from behind the eyes of a newborn baby, or barking at you from behind the counter at the Department of Motor Vehicles.

"This is all fine and well," you may be saying, "but I am also part of God's creation, so shouldn't I be included on the line that runs from bottom to top?" Well, yes, that is a very good point (or in this case, line). You will see that when we do this, when we include you not only on the line that moves from left to right, but also bottom to top, you will notice that when you encounter yourself—whether it be the face looking back at you in the mirror or the reflection of your soul against God's creation—you will find Christ.

- Where did you meet God today on your road to life?
- Breathe in the Our Father and meditate on the times you were aware that your life intersected with God.

Chapter 18

EDITING

S OME YEARS BACK, while fighting a bad case of insomnia, I switched on the TV and caught the tail end of a documentary about DVDs. In it, legendary film director Martin Scorsese talked about the importance of watching movies in widescreen as compared to full-screen formats. What's the difference? Well, Scorsese went on to say that when you watch movies on TV, normally you would see a disclaimer at the very beginning of the broadcast that says something like this: "This movie has been formatted to fit your screen." Since most people at the time of the documentary owned TVs that looked like boxes, this meant that a film shown in 35mm (which has a rectangular shape) in the movie theater, when shown on TV, literally had its left and right sides cut off. This meant that, on average, you were seeing only 70 percent of what the director had originally intended you to see.

If memory serves me here, I believe Scorsese went on to show a scene from *The Sound of Music* starring Julie Andrews. It was the opening scene when she twirls around in the Austrian Alps. Shown next to a clip that had been edited to fit the TV screen, you could definitely see a difference. In widescreen you watched the artist's intended vision. In TV full format, you missed out on some beautiful, intentional images that were essential to the viewer's experience.

He also compared scenes from his movie *Taxi Driver*, and on TV, during one pivotal sequence, you could see only Robert DeNiro up against a wall. In widescreen, you saw the actor against the wall, but you also saw the cops on the other side of the wall closing in on him.

This may have just been a well-done commercial to buy widescreen DVDs, but I don't think so. Scorcese talked with such passion about the disservice full format had done to movies, actors and directors, and to the viewers who watched the DVDs. Well, he had me sold and from then on I watched every movie I could in widescreen. Certainly, you had these black bands on the top and bottom of the screen, but you could watch the full picture, the full intention of the director.

The more I watched, the more I saw that Scorcese hadn't just been talking about movies, he had been talking about life as well. I had been doing a disservice to God's artistry. I began to see that, spiritually, I had cut off the ends of my experience. I could see in front of me, but that was it. I had spiritual myopia and was missing the beauty on the sides. How many people had I passed by on the street because all I did was see directly in front of me? How many people had I not helped? How many trees or signs had I walked past in my life?

Spiritual exercises, daily commitment to prayer and meditation, help us see in widescreen, help us see the panorama of God's creation, and help us see that, during those times when I think *God's not present in my full-format world,* all I need to do is pray. As the screen of my vision expands I see that God was standing there all along in the film of my life—I had just cut out the side he was standing on.

Scorcese Exercise

Close your eyes. Repeat the Jesus Prayer until you come to a relaxing place of quiet. In the darkness of your closed eyes, begin to roll film. Imagine that you are experiencing something important in your life. Maybe it's the birth of your child, your graduation, your first date. Create specific images in your mind. Try to expand your vision and see that experience in widescreen and imagine that God is there in the scene with you now, standing to the side, but in the event. He had been there all along, but those stupid TVs...

Part IV

EXERCISING WITH THE PARABLES

A question was proposed to a group: if God were a tree, what kind of tree would he be?

The people thought and after a few minutes of reflection, they began to speak, one at a time.

"God is a huge oak tree because God is strong and his roots are deep."

"God is a sycamore because I used to pray under one of those trees when I was a child."

"God is an elm tree because he gives me shade and because, well, I like elm trees."

"God is a weeping willow tree because the weeping willow is the most magnificent tree I've ever seen. There is one by a monastery near my home. On weekends in autumn, in the moments between night and dawn, I will walk to that field and enter into its canopy. I sit there on one of the long arms close to the ground and listen to the geese fly overhead."

"I'm from Arizona and there aren't many trees where I live. God is a cactus."

"In a book called *The Little Prince* there's a tree that's an entire world, and the Little Prince visits it. I always thought that was a beautiful image, a single giant tree on a tiny planet. Maybe that planet is heaven and all the angels live on its branches."

"I don't really like trees—all the leaves you have to clean up in the fall. God's not a tree to me."

"I know someone said that the weeping willow is the most magnificent tree in the world, but I'm assuming that's only because he's never seen a redwood. I was in that forest some years back and you'd be amazed at the size of these trees. I mean, they're as big as this room and some of them have been around for thousands of years. They stretch so high into the sky that you can't see where they end. That is God to me."

Christ was sitting in the room at the time, though no one knew it. When it was his turn to speak he said, "God for me is like the Charlie Brown Christmas tree."

"You mean that skinny little thing from the cartoon?" asked someone.

"Yes. For me, God is fragile and naked and most people pass him by without giving him much thought. The only people who seem to know the beauty that lies within are children who don't know any better."

"Good grief," moaned someone eating grapes.

Chapter 19

THE PARABLE OF THE
SOWER (DAY 1)

WHAT FOLLOWS is a seven-day spiritual exercise plan to illuminate the parables of Christ by incorporating variations of the Jesus Prayer, Centering Prayer, and Lectio Divina. Each day includes basic exercises, a reading from the Gospels, and questions for reflection, and each can be completed in less than fifteen minutes.

- Begin with an Our Father. When you have completed the prayer, focus your attention on the first word: *our*. Try not to think about it, but let it sit with you. How does it make you feel? How does that feeling relate to your life?
- Say the Jesus Prayer.
- Breathe in: "Lord Jesus Christ."
- Breathe out: "Have mercy on me."
- Repeat this prayer until you feel rested and focused and then move on to the day's first reading.

That same day Jesus went out of the house and sat by the lake. Such large crowds gathered around him that he got into a boat and sat in it, while all the people stood on the shore. Then he told them many things in parables, saying: "A farmer went out to sow his seed. As he was scattering the seed, some fell along the path, and the birds came and ate it up. Some fell on rocky places, where it did not have much soil. It sprang up quickly, because the soil was shallow. But when the sun came up, the plants were scorched, and they withered because they had no root. Other seed fell among thorns, which grew up and choked the plants. Still other seed fell on good soil, where it produced a crop—a hundred, sixty or thirty times what was sown. He who has ears, let him hear."

The disciples came to him and asked, "Why do you speak to the people in parables?" *(Matthew 13:1–10)*

Reflect
- What word stood out for you in the reading? Focus on that word and let it be with you. Repeat it and ask God for help in illuminating why that word struck a chord with you.
- Who is the sower? What are the seeds?
- Where in your life do you find healthy soil?
- How can you become healthy soil?

Chapter 20

THE PARABLE OF THE GREATEST IN THE KINGDOM OF HEAVEN (DAY 2)

- Begin by saying the Our Father. When you are done, focus on the word *father*. Let the word sit with you. What does *father* mean to you? Is your image of *father* one of comfort? If not, how does your relationship with your father affect the way you imagine God the Father to be?
- Repeat the Prayer of the Sacred Heart while consciously focusing on your breathing.
- Breathe in: "Sacred heart of Jesus."
- Breathe out: "I trust in thee."
- Repeat this until you feel relaxed and comforted and then move on to the day's reading.

At that time the disciples came to Jesus and asked, "Who is the greatest in the kingdom of heaven?"

He called a little child and had him stand among them. And he said: "I tell you the truth, unless you change and become like little children, you will never enter the kingdom of heaven. Therefore, whoever humbles himself like this child is the greatest in the kingdom of heaven."

(Matthew 18:1–4)

- What word stood out for you in the reading? Focus on that word and let it be with you. Repeat it and ask God for help in illuminating why that word struck a chord with you.

Chapter 21

THE PARABLE OF THE LOST SHEEP (DAY 3)

- Begin by saying the Our Father. When you have completed the prayer, focus on the word *who*. Who is God to you? Who is the Holy Spirit? Who is Christ? Meditate on Christ's words: "Who do you say I am?" Who are you?
- Repeat "Come, Holy Spirit, come." Breathe the words in and out. Feel the Holy Spirit rising inside you. Feel the power of God coursing through your body and soul and move on to your reading.

See that you do not look down on one of these little ones. For I tell you that their angels in heaven always see the face of my Father in heaven.

What do you think? If a man owns a hundred sheep, and one of them wanders away, will he not leave the ninety-nine on the hills and go to look for the one that wandered off? And if he finds it, I tell you the truth, he is happier about that one sheep than about the ninety-nine that did not wander off. In the same way your Father in heaven is not willing that any of these little ones should be lost. *(Matthew 18:10–14)*

- If we are all God's children, aren't we all "little ones"? If so, have you ever looked down on God's little ones? Why?
- Have you ever lost something and tried desperately to find it? Do you ever feel lost? Why?
- Do you believe God is searching for you? Ask God to help you be found.

Chapter 22

THE PARABLE OF THE UNMERCIFUL SERVANT (DAY 4)

- Begin with an Our Father. When you have completed the prayer, focus your attention on the words *who art in heaven*: Where can God be found in your life?
- Say the Jesus Prayer while consciously breathing in and out.
- Breathe in: "Lord Jesus Christ."
- Breathe out: "Have mercy on me."
- Repeat this prayer until you feel rested and focused and then move on to the day's first reading.

Then Peter came to Jesus and asked, "Lord, how many times shall I forgive my brother when he sins against me? Up to seven times?"

Jesus answered, "I tell you, not seven times, but seventy-seven times.

"Therefore, the kingdom of heaven is like a king who wanted to settle accounts with his servants. As he began the settlement, a man who owed him ten thousand talents was brought to him. Since he was not able to pay, the master ordered that he and his wife and his children and all that he had be sold to repay the debt.

"The servant fell on his knees before him. 'Be patient with me,' he begged, 'and I will pay back everything.' The servant's master took pity on him, canceled the debt and let him go.

"But when that servant went out, he found one of his fellow servants who owed him a hundred denarii. He grabbed him and began to choke him. 'Pay back what you owe me!' he demanded.

"His fellow servant fell to his knees and begged him, 'Be patient with me, and I will pay you back.'

"But he refused. Instead, he went off and had the man thrown into prison until he could pay the debt. When the other servants saw what had happened, they were greatly distressed and went and told their master everything that had happened.

"Then the master called the servant in. 'You wicked servant,' he said, 'I canceled all that debt of yours because you begged me to. Shouldn't you have had mercy on your fellow servant just as I had on you?' In anger his master turned him over to the jailers to be tortured, until he should pay back all he owed.

"This is how my heavenly Father will treat each of you unless you forgive your brother from your heart."

(Matthew 18:21–35)

- Focus on the line from the Our Father, "Forgive us our trespasses." Do you practice forgiveness? If so, how? Is there someone in your life that you haven't forgiven?
- Are you in need of forgiveness? Ask God for forgiveness and for the strength to forgive others—and yourself.

Chapter 23

THE PARABLE OF THE GOOD SAMARITAN (DAY 5)

- Begin by saying the Our Father. When you are done, focus on the word *father*. Let the word sit with you. What does *father* mean to you? Is your image of father one of comfort? If not, how does your relationship with your father affect the way you imagine God the Father to be?
- Repeat the Prayer of the Sacred Heart while consciously focusing on your breathing.
- Breathe in: "Sacred heart of Jesus."
- Breathe out: "I trust in thee."
- Repeat this until you feel relaxed and comforted and then move on to the day's reading.

On one occasion an expert in the law stood up to test Jesus. "Teacher," he asked, "what must I do to inherit eternal life?"

"What is written in the Law?" he replied. "How do you read it?"

He answered: "'Love the Lord your God with all your heart and with all your soul and with all your strength and with all your mind'; and, 'Love your neighbor as yourself.'"

"You have answered correctly," Jesus replied. "Do this and you will live."

But he wanted to justify himself, so he asked Jesus, "And who is my neighbor?"

In reply Jesus said: "A man was going down from Jerusalem to Jericho, when he fell into the hands of robbers. They stripped him of his clothes, beat him and went away, leaving him half dead. A priest happened to be going down the same road, and when he saw the man, he passed by on the other side. So too, a Levite, when he came to the place and saw him, passed by on the other side. But a Samaritan, as he traveled, came where the man was; and when he saw him, he took pity on him. He went to him and bandaged his wounds, pouring on oil and wine. Then he put the man on his own donkey, took him to an inn and took care of him. The next day he took out two silver coins and gave them to the innkeeper. 'Look after him,' he said, 'and when I return, I will reimburse you for any extra expense you may have.'

"Which of these three do you think was a neighbor to the man who fell into the hands of robbers?"

The expert in the law replied, "The one who had mercy on him."

Jesus told him, "Go and do likewise."

(Luke 10:25–37)

- When have you shown mercy to others? Who has shown mercy to you?
- How can you show mercy, not just to your family and friends, but to strangers as well? How can you "go and do likewise"?

Chapter 24

THE PARABLE OF
THE WORKERS IN
THE VINEYARD (DAY 6)

- Begin by saying the Our Father. When you have completed the prayer, focus on the word *hallowed*: Who is holy to you? What is holy to you?
- Repeat "Come, Holy Spirit, come." Breathe the words in and out of you. Feel the Holy Spirit rising inside you. Feel the power of God coursing through your body and soul and move on to your reading.

For the kingdom of heaven is like a landowner who went out early in the morning to hire men to work in his vineyard. He agreed to pay them a denarius for the day and sent them into his vineyard.

About the third hour he went out and saw others standing in the marketplace doing nothing. He told them,

"You also go and work in my vineyard, and I will pay you whatever is right." So they went.

He went out again about the sixth hour and the ninth hour and did the same thing. About the eleventh hour he went out and found still others standing around. He asked them, "Why have you been standing here all day long doing nothing?"

"Because no one has hired us," they answered.

He said to them, "You also go and work in my vineyard."

When evening came, the owner of the vineyard said to his foreman, "Call the workers and pay them their wages, beginning with the last ones hired and going on to the first."

The workers who were hired about the eleventh hour came and each received a denarius. So when those came who were hired first, they expected to receive more. But each one of them also received a denarius. When they received it, they began to grumble against the landowner. "These men who were hired last worked only one hour," they said, "and you have made them equal to us who have borne the burden of the work and the heat of the day."

But he answered one of them, "Friend, I am not being unfair to you. Didn't you agree to work for a denarius? Take your pay and go. I want to give the man who was hired last the same as I gave you. Don't I have the right to do what I want with my own money? Or are you envious because I am generous?"

So the last will be first, and the first will be last.

(Matthew 20:1–16)

- Do you live in an abundant world?
- Do you sometimes get angry at God's generosity to others? Do you ever feel slighted by God?
- How can you emulate the generosity of God in your life?

The Parable of the Workers [51]

Chapter 25

THE PARABLE OF THE LOST SON (DAY 7)

- Begin with an Our Father. When you have completed the prayer, focus your attention on the words *thy will be done*: What do these words mean to you?
- Say the Jesus Prayer while consciously breathing in and out.
- Breathe in: "Lord Jesus Christ."
- Breathe out: "Have mercy on me."
- Repeat this prayer until you feel rested and focused and then move on to the day's reading.

Jesus continued: "There was a man who had two sons. The younger one said to his father, 'Father, give me my share of the estate.' So he divided his property between them.

"Not long after that, the younger son got together all he had, set off for a distant country and there squandered his wealth in wild living. After he had spent everything, there was a severe famine in that whole country, and he began to be in need. So he went and hired himself out to a citizen of that country, who sent him to his fields to feed pigs. He longed to fill his stomach with the pods that the pigs were eating, but no one gave him anything.

"When he came to his senses, he said, 'How many of my father's hired men have food to spare, and here I am starving to death! I will set out and go back to my father and say to him: Father, I have sinned against heaven and against you. I am no longer worthy to be called your son; make me like one of your hired men.' So he got up and went to his father.

"But while he was still a long way off, his father saw him and was filled with compassion for him; he ran to his son, threw his arms around him and kissed him.

"The son said to him, 'Father, I have sinned against heaven and against you. I am no longer worthy to be called your son.'

"But the father said to his servants, 'Quick! Bring the best robe and put it on him. Put a ring on his finger and sandals on his feet. Bring the fattened calf and kill it. Let's have a feast and celebrate. For this son of mine was dead and is alive again; he was lost and is found.' So they began to celebrate.

"Meanwhile, the older son was in the field. When he came near the house, he heard music and dancing. So he called one of the servants and asked him what was going on. 'Your brother has come,' he replied, 'and your father has killed the fattened calf because he has him back safe and sound.'

"The older brother became angry and refused to go in. So his father went out and pleaded with him. But he answered his father, 'Look! All these years I've been slaving for you and never disobeyed your orders. Yet you never gave me even a young goat so I could celebrate with my friends. But when this son of yours who has squandered your property with prostitutes comes home, you kill the fattened calf for him!'

"'My son,' the father said, 'you are always with me, and everything I have is yours. But we had to celebrate and be glad, because this brother of yours was dead and is alive again; he was lost and is found.'"

(Luke 15:11–32)

- Which character in this story do you relate to the most: The lost son? The older brother? The father?
- Is this story fair? Have you ever felt like the older brother in this story, seemingly penalized or loved less because you had done the right thing while someone else goes off and does wrong?
- How can you reconcile this story with your life?

Part V

BRIDGING THE GAP

The old man and the boy were walking through a park.

"See those two trees over there?"

"Yes," said the boy.

"See the distance between them? See how their branches almost touch each other? *Almost,* but never do?"

"Yes."

"The tree on the left *adores* the tree on the right. And I'm pretty sure the tree on the right feels the same way about the tree on the left. They can't stop looking at each other. Did you hear what I said?"

"Yes," the boy answered.

The old man sighed. "No matter how much they yearn to be closer to each other they can never touch. They can never touch each other's happiness. They can never touch each other's suffering. If one gets sick, the other one can only watch, can't help. They are locked apart from each other forever."

"Unless lightning knocks one of them over onto the other," said the boy.

"Yes, you're right," said the old man. They stood together silently for a while. The wind blowing the branches of the trees. The old man smiled.

The boy looked up. "This makes me sad and angry," said the boy. "What are you smiling about?"

"Don't be sad," said the old man. "It's true that the branches of the trees can never touch. They can never hug. But if you go below the surface the roots of these two very separate trees are entwined and entangled. What they yearn for above, they experience deep below. We can't see it, but they share one life. What happens to one, happens to the other."

The boy thought for a moment and said, "I'm hungry."

"Me too. Let's go."

Chapter 26

THE STATIONS OF THE CROSS EXERCISES

I MAGINE for a moment the greatest love of your life: your beloved. This person is the center of your existence, a person who makes you feel truly alive. Before you met your beloved, you were anxious, you were distracted, you were frail, you were broken. But now in your emerging love, you feel strong, you feel human. You don't know what you were experiencing before, but it wasn't humanness. This person has helped you to understand your past and you are worrying less and less about the future. Instead you are focused on the here and now. Everything you do, everything you experience is saturated with true life.

Continue to imagine your beloved. This person is a gifted teacher and has not only taught you how to live your life but has also touched the hearts of a community. The more lives this person influences, the more people flock to your beloved looking for inspiration. This is certainly a drain on the time your beloved spends with you, but for the first time in your life you don't feel jealous. You begin to realize that the more love is shared, the more love you have in your life. If you had an apple and cut it in half and gave one piece of it to a stranger, you would have half of an apple to eat. You may get hungry. But if you give half of your love away, you end up having twice as much as you did in the first place. By giving away, you gain.

Though your beloved has helped numerous people, there are others who have grown bitter, envious, and angry. They slander your beloved. They criticize; they mock and soon bring your love to trial. Certainly, the storm clouds have been gathering. You heard the rumblings of discontent. Your beloved acknowledged that these were dangerous times. But everything moves so fast. One moment you are having dinner with your love and your friends and soon thereafter there are betrayals, an arrest, an indictment, torture, and a sentence of death. All in fewer than twenty-four hours.

Now imagine your world beginning to implode. Here is the love of your life, falsely accused and charged. Your beloved has committed no crime except to kick at a nest of sleeping hornets. "How people hate to be stirred from sleep!" you cry. You are helpless. You feel useless. There is nothing you can do. The people who have claimed loyalty to your beloved have turned their backs. You are not even allowed one final moment with your beloved. Instead you will be forced to be a spectator to this crime. You feel completely alone.

Shadows deepen. Winds hiss. The sky turns the color of used baptismal water. And in the arid air is the smell of death. A crowd starts to stir. You turn and you see in the distance your beloved looking snapped in two. Your love is now forced to walk in the streets among a jeering, spiteful crowd—laughter crackles like flames. On your beloved's back is the tool of execution. You cry out in horror, but your voice can not be heard.

The crowd is ravenous, held back by the arms of soldiers who have taken to the streets to keep the scene peaceful. Amid the chaos, a few people weep for your beloved, holding out their hands in support. You try to get closer to your love, moving among contorted faces, but the crowds are so deep. You catch a glimpse of your beloved struggling to walk. And then the falling. You want to help the love of your life, to ease the burden, to put an end to this madness.

But there is nothing you can do but watch and pray for mercy.

Then comes a whisper in your ear. "It is only when the seed is broken that the tree begins to grow."

The Stations of the Cross offer a way of walking in the footsteps of the Beloved. To walk through the stations is an examination, a journey of the soul, an exercise in being a witness, a supporter, a bearer of burden. In the Christian tradition, the Stations, also known as the Way of the Cross, are a sacred devotion that focuses on the Passion of Christ. Traditionally composed of fifteen events that trace the final path of Jesus' life—from the hours after the Last Supper up until his Resurrection—the Stations are a meditative prayer, a mystical pilgrimage into the suffering heart of Christ. They are, at their core, the story of Easter, which has at its center the story of a new exodus—a Moses-like movement out of myopic spiritual slavery into the panoramic promised land of love.

Popularized by the Franciscans in the thirteenth and fourteenth centuries, the custom of praying and meditating on the suffering of Christ probably dates back to the days following Christ's resurrection. Many stories have been passed down through the ages of followers of Jesus revisiting the sites where Christ walked in the final moments of his life. One such story contends that Mary, the mother of Jesus, was seen walking and praying in the footsteps of her beloved son, tracing his final journey from the Roman Praetorium, or Pilate's House, through the dry, cracked streets of Jerusalem to the place of the skull, Golgotha, where the blood of Christ mixed with the desert sands.

As this act of devotion grew in popularity and as Christianity spread across the Mediterranean and Europe, more and more people would set out on a pilgrimage to the Holy Land to walk in the footsteps of Christ. But as the Middles Ages dawned, Jerusalem became a very dangerous place. Many clergies began erecting symbolic stations in local churches so the faithful could stay close to home. The Stations of the Cross then became, literally, a series of paintings, illustrations, or sculptures that depicted the final scenes of Christ's earthly life. Though there were many variations on these events throughout the different communities—some were based on passages in the New Testament while others were popular stories that had been handed down from generation to generation—the Stations that most of the faithful have been reciting over the last four hundred years are these:

The Traditional Stations of the Cross
1. Jesus is condemned to death.
2. Jesus is made to carry the cross.
3. Jesus falls the first time.
4. Jesus is met by his mother.
5. Simon helps carry the cross.
6. Veronica wipes the face of Jesus.
7. Jesus falls the second time.
8. The women of Jerusalem mourn for Jesus.
9. Jesus falls the third time.

10. Jesus is stripped of his garments.
11. Jesus is nailed to the cross.
12. Jesus dies on the cross.
13. The body of Jesus is taken down from the cross.
14. The body of Jesus is laid in the tomb.
15. The resurrection.

In 1991, Pope John Paul II, wanting to give pilgrims and wayfarers an alternative set of Stations to pray and meditate on, proposed a new list based solely on events described in the New Testament. Gone were such episodes as Jesus encountering his mother on the way to his crucifixion, Veronica wiping the face of Christ, and the three falls.

The New Stations of the Cross

1. Jesus prays in the Garden of Olives.
2. Jesus is betrayed by Judas.
3. Jesus is condemned to death by the Sanhedrin.
4. Jesus is denied by Peter.
5. Jesus is judged by Pilate.
6. Jesus is scourged and crowned with thorns.
7. Jesus carries his cross.
8. Jesus is helped by Simon Cyrene.
9. Jesus encounters the women of Jerusalem.
10. Jesus is crucified.
11. Jesus promises to share his resurrection with the good thief.
12. Jesus is on the cross with his mother below him.
13. Jesus dies on the cross.
14. Jesus is placed in the tomb.
15. The resurrection.

Which set of Stations you choose to focus on is completely up to you.

The more you pray and meditate on the Stations, the more you'll realize that the very things we try to avoid in our lives are the places where God is most present. Well, let me rephrase that. God is always present in our lives, only sometimes our lack of awareness, our lack of vision, creates an illusion that he is hiding. Sure, it's easy to see God in a sunset when that sun isn't scorching our land or giving us cancer. It is easy to see God in nature when nature isn't trying to sting us or flood our cities. It's easy to see God in a newborn baby, when that baby isn't crying at 3:00 AM.

Yet God is ever present in the easy *and* the difficult, in the beautiful and the ugly. But there are moments in life when it is very hard to find God and very easy to think God doesn't exist, to feel abandoned and alone. It is in these less-than-obvious places that the Stations can take us to another level of understanding and commitment.

The Stations of the Cross are about finding God where you least expect him.

When we were first married, my bride and I were renting out the first floor of a split-level house. We were living on a quiet cul-de-sac in a suburban neighborhood. During this time a homeless man roamed the streets during the day, collecting cans and going through everyone's trash on garbage days. When I first saw him, I was a bit startled, but after a while it seemed that this man had become a fixture in the neighborhood and that people actually separated their recyclables for him. We began doing the same. This went on for a few months. I'd see him in the mornings as I was walking to the train to commute into the city and sometimes at night walking up and down the road that ran parallel to the rails. He never bothered anyone and eventually he became a strange staple in our lives.

One day, though, as I was leaving to go to work, I found him in our driveway. It wasn't garbage day. For the first time I saw this man deliberately step over this imaginary boundary that we—and the neighborhood—had created. It was one thing to go through trash when it was at the curb, but here he was literally on my property. He had crossed the line.

"What are you doing?" I asked.

No response.

I spoke more loudly: "What are you doing?"

Still, no response.

Infuriated, I repeated myself a third time: "What are you doing?"

Without looking up, he said, "I'm searching for God."

For a moment, I was stunned. That was not at all what I was expecting him to say. I grew angry and felt rage swell up inside of me. I felt insulted for myself and for that pharisaical moment of self-righteousness, for God.

Now, I consider myself a spiritual person. I also consider myself patient and kind. But maybe not, because I screamed at him, "Get out of here!"

He kept picking through the trash and as I started to move closer to him, he picked something out of the garbage. I couldn't see what. Slowly he walked to the curb, gathered up his bag and cart, and walked away as if nothing had happened.

I was filled with anger and fear.

That week I waited for him to show up again. He didn't. I looked for him the following week and he never appeared. That incident in front of the house was the last time I ever saw the man.

Over the years, I have thought about that incident many times, wondering what had happened to him. What did he pull out of the garbage? Where had he gone? Was he arrested? Did he get hit by a car? Did he die? And then his words. His words left an indelible scratch on my soul: "I'm searching for God."

As time has passed, I see that incident as another gift from God. If you had asked me then where I think God could be found, I would have said "All around me," but I wouldn't have been telling you the truth. I never would have thought to say that God was in my garbage can. Yet, if God creates all things, then he must be contained in all the things of the world, even the things that we throw away, even the things we want to get rid of like pain and suffering and anger.

That man taught me the key to understanding the Passion of Christ, which in turn is the key to understanding the Stations of the Cross. It is in the throwaways of life — the people we ignore and the things we want to get rid of, like loneliness and disillusionment, where God can be most easily found.

Preparation for Stations of the Cross Exercise

From time to time give one percent of your day to the Stations of the Cross. Start by focusing on your breathing and read the first Scripture passage that follows (both sets of Stations are included in the pages ahead). Begin tracing the steps of the Passion, allowing yourself to enter the scene through your imagination. Maybe you are a bystander, Christ's friend, his mother, or imagine that you are Christ yourself.

- What do you see?
- What are the sounds you hear?
- What are you feeling?
- What do you smell?
- What do you taste in the air?
- How does Christ's passion affect you today? Does it? Should it?
- What is your cross to bear?
- Ask the Holy Spirit for help to lift the weight.

Chapter 27

THE TRADITIONAL STATIONS
OF THE CROSS

The First Station:
Jesus Is Condemned to Death

Now it was the governor's custom at the Feast to release a prisoner chosen by the crowd. At that time they had a notorious prisoner, called Barabbas. So when the crowd had gathered, Pilate asked them, "Which one do you want me to release to you: Barabbas, or Jesus who is called Christ?" For he knew it was out of envy that they had handed Jesus over to him.

While Pilate was sitting on the judge's seat, his wife sent him this message: "Don't have anything to do with that innocent man, for I have suffered a great deal today in a dream because of him."

But the chief priests and the elders persuaded the crowd to ask for Barabbas and to have Jesus executed.

"Which of the two do you want me to release to you?" asked the governor.

"Barabbas," they answered.

"What shall I do, then, with Jesus who is called Christ?" Pilate asked.

They all answered, "Crucify him!"

(Matthew 27:15–22)

Reflect
- Imagine that you are one of the people in crowd. What are you feeling as you witness Christ being judged this way?
- When in your life have you followed the crowd instead of following the inner voice that is God?

The Second Station:
Jesus Carries His Cross

Then the governor's soldiers took Jesus into the Praetorium and gathered the whole company of soldiers around him. They stripped him and put a scarlet robe on him, and then twisted together a crown of thorns and set it on his head. They put a staff in his right hand and knelt in front of him and mocked him. "Hail, king of the Jews!" they said. They spit on him, and took the staff and struck him on the head again and again. After they had mocked him, they took off the robe and put his own clothes on him. Then they led him away to crucify him.

(Matthew 27:27–31)

Reflect
- Imagine that you are Christ as he's mocked and abused by Roman soldiers. Imagine the pain he must have suffered and the humiliation he must have felt at the hands of these people. Imagine the blows. Imagine the spit in his face. Imagine being struck in the head repeatedly.
- What do you see? How do you feel? What are you thinking?

The Third Station:
Jesus Falls for the First Time

How long, O LORD? Will you forget me forever?
How long will you hide your face from me?
How long must I wrestle with my thoughts
and every day have sorrow in my heart?
How long will my enemy triumph over me?
Look on me and answer, O LORD my God.
Give light to my eyes, or I will sleep in death;
my enemy will say, "I have overcome him,"
and my foes will rejoice when I fall.
But I trust in your unfailing love;
my heart rejoices in your salvation.
I will sing to the LORD,
for he has been good to me. (Psalm 13:1–6)

Reflect
- Imagine watching Christ fall because he is so weak and filled with burden. How can you help God alleviate the burdens of others?
- Have you ever felt as if God has abandoned you? How did that make you feel? How did this affect your faith? Did your faith grow stronger through these experiences?
- Do you trust in God's unfailing love? Are there times when you doubt that love? Why?

The Fourth Station:
Jesus Meets His Mother

Then Simeon blessed them and said to Mary, his mother: "This child is destined to cause the falling and rising of many in Israel, and to be a sign that will be spoken against, so that the thoughts of many hearts will be revealed. And a sword will pierce your own soul too." *(Luke 2:34–35)*

Reflect
- Imagine you are the mother of Christ. What do you feel as you watch your son being led to his death?
- What do you want to do as the scene unfolds? Are you angry at God for allowing this to happen?

The Fifth Station:
Simon of Cyrene Helps Carry the Cross

As they led him away, they seized Simon from Cyrene, who was on his way in from the country, and put the cross on him and made him carry it behind Jesus. A large number of people followed him, including women who mourned and wailed for him. *(Luke 23:26–27)*

Reflect
- Imagine that you are the bystander Simon. What do you experience as you watch this man suffer? What does this condemned man look like? What do you feel for him? How heavy is the cross you are helping to carry?
- When in your life have you helped someone carry a burden? How did you help? How did this change your life? Are there people in your life now who need assistance carrying their crosses? How can you help them now?

The Sixth Station:
Veronica Wipes the Face of Jesus

Restore us, O God; make your face shine upon us, that we may be saved. *(Psalm 80:3)*

Reflect
- Imagine you are looking into the eyes of the Christ. What do they look like? What do you see?
- Have you ever seen the face of Christ in another? What did you experience, and how did it affect your faith?

The Seventh Station:
Jesus Falls the Second Time

If the LORD delights in a man's way,
he makes his steps firm;
though he stumble, he will not fall,
for the LORD upholds him with his hand.
                    (Psalm 37:23–24)

Reflect
- When have you stumbled in your life? When have you stumbled in your faith? Did you feel the hand of God trying to help you up?
- Memorize this psalm and use it as a prayer when you are struggling with a relationship, a job, a memory, an illness.

The Eighth Station:
Jesus Meets the Women of Jerusalem

Jesus turned and said to them, "Daughters of Jerusalem, do not weep for me; weep for yourselves and for your children. For the time will come when you will say, 'Blessed are the barren women, the wombs that never bore and the breasts that never nursed!' Then they will say to the mountains, 'Fall on us!' and to the hills, 'Cover us!' For if men do these things when the tree is green, what will happen when it is dry?" *(Luke 23:28–31)*

Reflect
- These are strong words from Christ. What do they mean to you?
- Do you feel we are in a "green" or "dry" period in history?
- How can you, with the power of the Holy Spirit, help transform the crying of this world to jubilation?

The Ninth Station:
Jesus Falls the Third Time

The LORD upholds all those who fall and lifts up all who are bowed down. *(Psalm 145:14)*

Reflect
- When have you fallen in your life and how has God raised you up?
- How can you raise God up in your life?

The Tenth Station:
Jesus Is Stripped of His Garments

They took his clothes, dividing them into four shares, one for each of them, with the undergarment remaining. This garment was seamless, woven in one piece from top to bottom.

"Let's not tear it," they said to one another. "Let's decide by lot who will get it."

This happened that the scripture might be fulfilled that said,

"They divided my clothes among them and cast lots for my garment." *(John 19:23–24)*

Reflect
- What is the significance of the seamless garment? How have we stripped God in our lives?
- When have you felt bare and exposed in your life? How did it make you feel?

The Eleventh Station:
Jesus Is Nailed to the Cross

They brought Jesus to the place called Golgotha (which means The Place of the Skull). Then they offered him wine mixed with myrrh, but he did not take it. And they crucified him.... They crucified two robbers with him, one on his right and one on his left. Those who passed by hurled insults at him, shaking their heads and saying, "So! You who are going to destroy the temple and build it in three days, come down from the cross and save yourself!"
(Mark 15:22–30)

Reflect
- Imagine you are Christ dying on the cross. What do you feel? What is going through your mind?
- How do we crucify God in our lives? How do we crucify each other?

The Twelfth Station:
Jesus Dies on the Cross

At the sixth hour darkness came over the whole land until the ninth hour. And at the ninth hour Jesus cried out in a loud voice, "Eloi, Eloi, lama sabachthani?" — which means, "My God, my God, why have you forsaken me?"

When some of those standing near heard this, they said, "Listen, he's calling Elijah."

One man ran, filled a sponge with wine vinegar, put it on a stick, and offered it to Jesus to drink. "Now leave him alone. Let's see if Elijah comes to take him down," he said.

With a loud cry, Jesus breathed his last.

(Mark 15:33–37)

Reflect
- Why does Christ call out, "My God, my God, why have you forsaken me"? Do you believe Christ believed his Father had abandoned him?
- Have there been times in your life when you feel God has abandoned you? Have you ever abandoned a loved one? A coworker? A stranger?

The Thirteenth Station:
Jesus Is Taken Down from the Cross

Joseph of Arimathea, a prominent member of the Council, who was himself waiting for the kingdom of God, went boldly to Pilate and asked for Jesus' body. Pilate was surprised to hear that he was already dead. Summoning the centurion, he asked him if Jesus had already died. When he learned from the centurion that it was so, he gave the body to Joseph. *(Mark 15:43–45)*

Reflect
- How can you carry the body of Christ in your life?

The Fourteenth Station:
Jesus Is Buried in the Tomb

So Joseph bought some linen cloth, took down the body, wrapped it in the linen, and placed it in a tomb cut out of rock. Then he rolled a stone against the entrance of the tomb. Mary Magdalene and Mary the mother of Joses saw where he was laid. *(Mark 15:46–47)*

Reflect
- Imagine that you are walking with Mary Magdalene, Mary, and Joseph. What are you feeling as you stand before the tomb?

The Fifteenth Station:
The Resurrection

After the Sabbath, at dawn on the first day of the week, Mary Magdalene and the other Mary went to look at the tomb.

There was a violent earthquake, for an angel of the Lord came down from heaven and, going to the tomb, rolled back the stone and sat on it. His appearance was like lightning, and his clothes were white as snow. The guards were so afraid of him that they shook and became like dead men.

The angel said to the women, "Do not be afraid, for I know that you are looking for Jesus, who was crucified. He is not here; he has risen, just as he said. Come and see the place where he lay. Then go quickly and tell his disciples: 'He has risen from the dead and is going ahead of you into Galilee. There you will see him.' Now I have told you." *(Matthew 28:1–7)*

Reflect
- Imagine you are with Mary Magdalene as she looks in the tomb. Imagine you see a figure in white telling you that Christ has risen from the dead. What does this mean to you? What do you feel? What is the expression on Mary's face? Are you filled with happiness? Disbelief?
- What is the significance of the resurrection in your life?

Chapter 28

THE NEW STATIONS
OF THE CROSS

The First Station:
The Agony of Jesus in the Garden

Then Jesus went with his disciples to a place called Gethsemane, and he said to them, "Sit here while I go over there and pray." He took Peter and the two sons of Zebedee along with him, and he began to be sorrowful and troubled. Then he said to them, "My soul is overwhelmed with sorrow to the point of death. Stay here and keep watch with me."

Going a little farther, he fell with his face to the ground and prayed, "My Father, if it is possible, may this cup be taken from me. Yet not as I will, but as you will."

(Matthew 26:36–39)

Reflect

- Imagine you are Christ in the garden. Imagine what he must have felt during this period of prayer. Imagine the feeling of the air on your hands and lips as you lift your hands to God and pray for your cup to be taken from you. What is your will?

The Second Station:
The Betrayal and Arrest of Jesus

While he was still speaking, Judas, one of the Twelve, arrived. With him was a large crowd armed with swords and clubs, sent from the chief priests and the elders of the people. Now the betrayer had arranged a signal with them: "The one I kiss is the man; arrest him." Going at once to Jesus, Judas said, "Greetings, Rabbi!" and kissed him.

Jesus replied, "Friend, do what you came for."

Then the men stepped forward, seized Jesus and arrested him. *(Matthew 26:47–50)*

Reflect
- When have you betrayed another? When have you been betrayed? Pray for forgiveness and for the strength to forgive another.

The Third Station:
Jesus Is Condemned by the Sanhedrin

The chief priests and the whole Sanhedrin were looking for false evidence against Jesus so that they could put him to death. But they did not find any, though many false witnesses came forward.

Finally two came forward and declared, "This fellow said, 'I am able to destroy the temple of God and rebuild it in three days.'"

Then the high priest stood up and said to Jesus, "Are you not going to answer? What is this testimony that these men are bringing against you?" But Jesus remained silent.

The high priest said to him, "I charge you under oath by the living God: Tell us if you are the Christ, the Son of God."

"Yes, it is as you say," Jesus replied. "But I say to all of you: In the future you will see the Son of Man sitting at the right hand of the Mighty One and coming on the clouds of heaven."

Then the high priest tore his clothes and said, "He has spoken blasphemy! Why do we need any more witnesses? Look, now you have heard the blasphemy. What do you think?"

"He is worthy of death," they answered.

(Matthew 26:59–66)

Reflect

- How do we condemn the people around us? Have you ever felt self-righteous toward another?
- Have you ever experienced the self-righteousness of others? How did this make you feel?
- Have you ever felt self-righteous in the name of God?

The Fourth Station:
Peter Denies Jesus

Now Peter was sitting out in the courtyard, and a servant girl came to him. "You also were with Jesus of Galilee," she said.

But he denied it before them all. "I don't know what you're talking about," he said.

Then he went out to the gateway, where another girl saw him and said to the people there, "This fellow was with Jesus of Nazareth."

He denied it again, with an oath: "I don't know the man!"

After a little while, those standing there went up to Peter and said, "Surely you are one of them, for your accent gives you away."

Then he began to call down curses on himself and he swore to them, "I don't know the man!"

Immediately a rooster crowed. Then Peter remembered the word Jesus had spoken: "Before the rooster crows, you will disown me three times." And he went outside and wept bitterly. *(Matthew 26:69–75)*

Reflect

- What is the essential difference between Judas, who betrayed Christ once, and Peter, who denied him three times?
- Have you ever denied someone out of fear? How do we deny the humanity of our fellow human beings? What can you do through the Holy Spirit to change that?

The Fifth Station:
Pilate Condemns Jesus to the Cross

Now it was the governor's custom at the Feast to release a prisoner chosen by the crowd. At that time they had a notorious prisoner, called Barabbas. So when the crowd had gathered, Pilate asked them, "Which one do you want me to release to you: Barabbas, or Jesus who is called Christ?" For he knew it was out of envy that they had handed Jesus over to him.

While Pilate was sitting on the judge's seat, his wife sent him this message: "Don't have anything to do with that innocent man, for I have suffered a great deal today in a dream because of him."

But the chief priests and the elders persuaded the crowd to ask for Barabbas and to have Jesus executed.

"Which of the two do you want me to release to you?" asked the governor.

"Barabbas," they answered.

"What shall I do, then, with Jesus who is called Christ?" Pilate asked.

They all answered, "Crucify him!"

"Why? What crime has he committed?" asked Pilate.

But they shouted all the louder, "Crucify him!"

When Pilate saw that he was getting nowhere, but that instead an uproar was starting, he took water and washed his hands in front of the crowd. "I am innocent of this man's blood," he said. "It is your responsibility!"

(Matthew 27:15–24)

Reflect

• What is your responsibility to God?
• What is your responsibility to God's creation?

The Sixth Station:
Jesus Is Scourged and Crowned with Thorns

Then the governor's soldiers took Jesus into the Praetorium and gathered the whole company of soldiers around him. They stripped him and put a scarlet robe on him, and then twisted together a crown of thorns and set it on his head. They put a staff in his right hand and knelt in front of him and mocked him. "Hail, king of the Jews!" they said. They spit on him, and took the staff and struck him on the head again and again. *(Matthew 27:27–30)*

Reflect

• Imagine that you are Christ in front of the Roman soldiers. What are you feeling? Fear? Anger? Sadness? Defiance?

The Seventh Station:
Jesus Is Mocked by the Soldiers and Given His Cross

After they had mocked him, they took off the robe and put his own clothes on him. Then they led him away to crucify him. *(Matthew 27:31)*

Reflect
- Have you ever been mocked? How did it make you feel?
- Have you ever mocked another?

The Eighth Station:
Simon the Cyrenian Helps Jesus Carry His Cross

As they were going out, they met a man from Cyrene, named Simon, and they forced him to carry the cross.
(Matthew 27:32)

Reflect
- How can you help a loved one, a stranger, a coworker carry his cross in life?

The Ninth Station:
Jesus Meets the Women of Jerusalem

A large number of people followed him, including women who mourned and wailed for him. Jesus turned and said to them, "Daughters of Jerusalem, do not weep for me; weep for yourselves and for your children."

(Luke 23:27–28)

Reflect
- What is the meaning of Christ's words here? Why does he not want these women's tears?
- Why should they cry for their own children?

The Tenth Station:
Jesus Is Crucified

They came to a place called Golgotha (which means The Place of the Skull). There they offered Jesus wine to drink, mixed with gall; but after tasting it, he refused to drink it. When they had crucified him, they divided up his clothes by casting lots. And sitting down, they kept watch over him there. *(Matthew 27:33–37)*

Reflect
- Imagine you are sitting at the foot of the cross keeping watch over Christ. What do you feel as you look at this man dying before you?

The Eleventh Station:
Jesus Promises Paradise to the Penitent Criminal

Two other men, both criminals, were also led out with him to be executed. When they came to the place called the Skull, there they crucified him, along with the criminals—one on his right, the other on his left. Jesus said, "Father, forgive them, for they do not know what they are doing." And they divided up his clothes by casting lots.

The people stood watching, and the rulers even sneered at him. They said, "He saved others; let him save himself if he is the Christ of God, the Chosen One...."

One of the criminals who hung there hurled insults at him: "Aren't you the Christ? Save yourself and us!"

But the other criminal rebuked him. "Don't you fear God," he said, "since you are under the same sentence? We are punished justly, for we are getting what our deeds deserve. But this man has done nothing wrong."

Then he said, "Jesus, remember me when you come into your kingdom."

Jesus answered him, "I tell you the truth, today you will be with me in paradise." *(Luke 23:32–43)*

Reflect

- Imagine you are one of the two criminals who are being crucified with Christ. Which one did you choose? What do you say to Christ?
- Continue the conversation. What would you say to Christ as you were suffering with him?

The Twelfth Station:
Jesus Speaks to His Mother and to His Disciple

Near the cross of Jesus stood his mother, his mother's sister, Mary the wife of Clopas, and Mary Magdalene. When Jesus saw his mother there, and the disciple whom he loved standing nearby, he said to his mother, "Dear woman, here is your son," and to the disciple, "Here is your mother." From that time on, this disciple took her into his home. *(John 19:25–27)*

Reflect
- What is the significance of Christ's words?
- How are we to protect those God loves?

The Thirteenth Station:
Jesus Dies on the Cross

From the sixth hour until the ninth hour darkness came over all the land. About the ninth hour Jesus cried out in a loud voice, "Eloi, Eloi, lama sabachthani?" — which means, "My God, my God, why have you forsaken me?"

When some of those standing there heard this, they said, "He's calling Elijah."

Immediately one of them ran and got a sponge. He filled it with wine vinegar, put it on a stick, and offered it to Jesus to drink. The rest said, "Now leave him alone. Let's see if Elijah comes to save him."

And when Jesus had cried out again in a loud voice, he gave up his spirit. *(Matthew 27:45–50)*

Reflect
• Meditate on the words "My God, my God, why have you forsaken me?" What do these words mean to you?

The Fourteenth Station:
The Burial of Jesus

As evening approached, there came a rich man from Arimathea, named Joseph, who had himself become a disciple of Jesus. Going to Pilate, he asked for Jesus' body, and Pilate ordered that it be given to him. Joseph took the body, wrapped it in a clean linen cloth, and placed it in his own new tomb that he had cut out of the rock. He rolled a big stone in front of the entrance to the tomb and went away. Mary Magdalene and the other Mary were sitting there opposite the tomb. *(Matthew 27:57–61)*

Reflect
- Have you ever rolled a stone in front of your heart? Have you ever blocked God from coming into your life?

The Fifteenth Station:
The Resurrection

After the Sabbath, at dawn on the first day of the week, Mary Magdalene and the other Mary went to look at the tomb.

There was a violent earthquake, for an angel of the Lord came down from heaven and, going to the tomb, rolled back the stone and sat on it. His appearance was like lightning, and his clothes were white as snow. The guards were so afraid of him that they shook and became like dead men.

The angel said to the women, "Do not be afraid, for I know that you are looking for Jesus, who was crucified. He is not here; he has risen, just as he said. Come and see the place where he lay. Then go quickly and tell his disciples: 'He has risen from the dead and is going ahead of you into Galilee. There you will see him.' Now I have told you."

So the women hurried away from the tomb, afraid yet filled with joy, and ran to tell his disciples. Suddenly Jesus met them. "Greetings," he said. They came to him, clasped his feet and worshiped him. Then Jesus said to them, "Do not be afraid. Go and tell my brothers to go to Galilee; there they will see me." *(Matthew 28:1–10)*

Reflect
- Christ says, "Do not be afraid." Meditate on these words and breathe them in and out as a silent prayer. What do these words mean to you? Do they bring you comfort?
- How can you help Christ continue the miracle of his resurrection in the lives of those around you?

Part VI

CODA

Some years back I was walking on a narrow cobblestone street off Boulevard Saint-Germain in Paris when I noticed a scruffy-looking individual kneeling in front of a café. He seemed to be praying, or begging inventively. He appeared to be in his forties and was dressed in black pants and a white shirt. His beard was unkempt, but his hair, which was thinning on top, was handsomely combed. His eyes were closed tight. His hands were clasped together and he gently rocked back and forth.

I remember it was late in the afternoon and the city streets and cafés were beginning to fill with twilight tourists and crepuscular light. No one seemed to be paying this man any attention and I certainly wasn't going to. But all my life I have been a magnet for misfits, madmen, and mendicants, and just as I was about to turn my gaze away, he opened his eyes, stared right at me, winked, and gave me an I'm-going-to-ask-you-for-money-smile. He jumped to his feet with the athleticism of a young man, said something to me in French, and genuflected before me.

"I'm sorry, I don't speak French," I said.

"Ah, Americaaan," he replied, standing up again quickly and putting out his hand.

I shook it. Calloused and strong. "Yes," I said.

"Me!" Slapping his hands on his chest, he said, "I lived in Brooklyn for seven years with my brother until he died."

When he said the word *died*, he clasped his hands, raised them to heaven, and said something again in French.

"I'm sorry," I said.

"What is your name?" he asked. His accent was French, but his English was perfect.

I told him.

"Allow me to introduce myself. I am the Brain," he said, bowing again to expose the large bald spot on the crown of his head. There was a scab in the center.

"The Brain?"

"Yes, I am the Brain because I am thinking the world into a new existence." He pointed to his head. "With my brain!"

"Is that how you hurt yourself?" I asked, pointing to the drying wound.

"Ah," he said, stroking the side of his head. "Sometimes the spirit is so powerful I fall down!"

"What spirit are you talking about?" I asked.

He stuck out his chest, placed one hand on his heart, and raised his other high, pointing to the darkening sky. "I have not had a drink since my brother died seven years ago! I am talking about the Holy Spirit! The Holy Spirit! The Spirit that flows through you and me!"

I apologized to him and tried to walk around him.

"Do you pray?"

"I do," I replied.

"I pray all the time! When I am walking, when I am thinking, when I am eating, when I am sleeping, when I am falling." He took a step closer to me, looked over his shoulder, and whispered in my face, "I am praying right now."

He may not have drank, but he certainly smelled like cigarettes and was in need of a bath.

"Brain," I said, gently slapping him on the chest, "I rename
you Brother Lawrence!"

"Brother Lawrence?"

"Yes, he was a monk who turned his life into a perpetual
prayer. Everything he did he believed was a prayer. If he washed a
dish, he offered that moment up to God."

He raised both arms in the air and his smile seemed to eclipse
his face. He was missing two teeth. "I am Brother Lawrence, the
Brain! I am thinking the world into existence! With my brain!"

I had not wanted to talk to the man when he first locked his
"gaze" on me, but now, I had to admit, I was intrigued. Nonethe-
less, I checked for my wallet in my pocket and asked him a question. "How are you going to do that, Brother Lawrence?"

"By praying!" He jumped up and down and started to dance
in place.

"And your prayers are going to change the world?" I ques-
tioned.

"They already have."

We talked for a few more minutes. About Brooklyn and Coney
Island, about his brother, a janitor who died from cancer. About
love, booze, cigarettes, Christ, the Virgin Mary, but mostly about
the Holy Spirit.

I had quickly grown fond of the man, but it was getting late
and I wanted to leave and walk on into the growing night.

"Can I have your cigarettes in your pocket?"

"Sure," I said and gave him the pack. Brown-papered Nat
Shermans from the old store on 42nd Street in New York City. I
don't smoke anymore.

"I have something for you," he said.

"What is that, Brother Lawrence?"

"It is this." He bent down and on the ground was an artist's paintbrush. He put it in my hand. His eyes narrowed and while I don't remember exactly what he said, he whispered a story that went something like this:

"This looks like an ordinary paintbrush anyone could buy, but this particular brush has a long and colorful history, of which you are now a part. Originally bought in Cleveland, Ohio, by a mother for her twenty-two-year-old son with dreams of being a world-renowned artist, the brush traveled in the young man's valise, first on a Greyhound bus from Lake Erie Downtown Station to New York City. From there, Henri (for this was the young man's name) departed for Paris, flying nonstop from JFK to Charles de Gaulle Airport. It was while studying under the auspices of the International Council for the Preservation of the Humanities that the young man met Antoine, a young vine grower from the Loire Valley with the uncanny ability of changing wine into water.

"Miracle? You may think so. 'A curse,' he called it. They became friends and drank Evian out of burgundy bottles on the banks of the Seine while pontificating on the role of the artist in society. It was during a night of drunken tomfoolery that the young man's favorite paintbrush, which he always carried with him in the breast pocket of an old coat his father used to wear, was lost during a scuffle with some local boys from the Nord.

"Lying in the street for days, it was eventually picked up by a vagrant street magician known in the cafés along Saint-Germain as Revoltaire. He used the brush as a disappointing substitute for the Magic Wand of Havana, a gift from his illusionist step-brother in Cuba, to perform his bits of sleight of hand and chicanery. While trying unsuccessfully to turn a belt into a spotted snake for a group of college students from Australia, this 'Street Christ' (as he was called by his one friend, Father Marcel of Notre Dame de Déception) lost his patience and threw the brush back into the street where it was eventually picked up by a monkey named Pascal.

"Pascal's master, a one-handed accordionist and displaced Irishman named McGreevy, used the paintbrush on occasion as a conductor's baton when he whistled the melody of Edith Piaf's 'L'Effet Que Tu Me Fais' (the only Piaf song he knew by heart) while Pascal danced his primitive ballet in the streets of the Latin Quarter for loose francs (this was before the currency switched to euros). One night, as McGreevy and Pascal were walking home (home was a small studio above a chicken house in Montmarte), the brush fell out of a plastic bag and rolled down the long, steep stairs photographed by countless romantics and known as the Stairway of Lovers, near Sacré Coeur. Having traveled nearly 150 steps, the brush at full velocity hit a high bump in a cobblestone street and landed in a crate of blank videotapes that were being loaded onto a truck, which was heading to the South of France for the Cannes Film Festival.

"Once the brush made it to the Riviera, it traveled through parts of Switzerland and Italy, carried for a time by the Seven Wandering Jews of Bratislava who had made a wrong turn in Slovakia. Then it changed hands from a pastry chef to a beautiful schoolteacher named Maman to a young crippled violinist named Sophie to an old olive farmer in Sicily named Leo. From there it passed through several more hands—many with arthritis, moles, dry skin, broken fingernails, and gaudy gold rings—and landed in North Africa, where it fell into the possession of a group of Bedouins who mixed cactus wine with the dust of ancient pulverized stars and used the brush to paint astrological charts on the skins of dead camels.

"Unfortunately—for these creations were reported to be the work of the great, great, great, great, great, great, great, great, great, great, great grandson of one of the Magi who visited Christ at his birth—the brush was stolen by a gypsy bandit as the Bedouins were trading their desert finds at an oasis for cans of sardines and chick peas. It did, however, soon find its way to me. What transpired between myself and the gypsy bandit, I cannot tell you, but you see now that we are all connected, by life, by death, by this brush. I am giving it to you. It is yours and it beckons you to paint!"

I stood with my mouth open and if it had been a hot midsummer night, not a cool April evening, I'm sure a fly could have flown down my throat.

"I'm speechless. I don't know what to say."

"Say nothing," he said. "Paint!"

"I can't paint. I'm a writer."

"You will paint my story with words then," he said.

"No one would believe it," I said.

"Then paint words about prayer," he said.

I looked at the brush and at the eyes of this enflamed soul.

"I promise," I said.

"I am Brother Lawrence," he said, dancing. "The Brain. I am thinking the world into existence. With my brain!"

I shook his hand and he hugged me—a strange-smelling bear. I said good-bye and walked off into the night.

A few blocks away I could have sworn I heard him call out: "Remember! Prayer!" But I couldn't be sure. I like to think I did.

Along my walk I passed a couple sitting on the steps of a church kissing in the blue light of a spring night in Paris. I laid the brush at their feet, took out a pen, and in the small notebook I always carried with me I wrote—or should I say, painted—two words: *Pray always.*

Brother Lawrence, the Brain, I have painted this book for you.

May God keep you safe.

ACKNOWLEDGMENTS

To Joseph P. Minasi, for finding my flash drive with my manuscript on it on a seat on the LIRR and returning it to me, I owe you my eternal gratitude.

To Meredith Smith, thank you for believing in this project and for believing in me. This book lives because of you.

To Michelle Rapkin, my editor and friend, thank you for your support and for taking this project by the hand and leading it where it needed to go.

To my agent, Victoria Skurnick, one of the great loves of my life, thank you for your patience, tenacity, friendship and your power to scare and motivate me at the same time.

To Jennifer Stallone Riddell, thank you for your friendship all these years and for being one of my biggest supporters. I feel truly blessed to know you and even though you are thousands of miles away your influence is felt every day.

To Jessie Sayward Bright, your kindness, sensitivity and presence helped shaped this book in unexpected ways. I thank you for being a part of my life and for inspiring me.

To Eric Hafker and Michael Stephenson, the poetry of your

friendship makes my world a much more beautiful place. We are and always will be brothers in arms.

To Trace Murphy, Darya Porat, Talia Krohn, Michael Palgon, John Burke, Roger Scholl, Anna Thompson, and Phillip Patrick, thank you for your thoughtfulness, support and kindness. I am very fortunate and blessed to know and work with all of you.

To the following people for their dedication and support, you have my endless gratitude: Rolf Zettersten, Harry Helm, Holly Halverson, Peggy Boelke, Erin Miner, Amanda Brown, Jody Waldrup, Andrea Kellner, Veronica Sepe, Adlai Yeomans, Bob Castillo, Dan Kendall, Gerry O'Collins, Jeff LaBelle, Brad Miner, Jon Sweeney, Tom Craughwell, Raymond Arroyo, Marcus Grodi, Paul Moses, James P. Moore, Scott Hahn, Mike Aquilina, Father Bob Barron, Nancy Ross, Jim Martin, Paul Coutinho, Greg Cootsona, Greg Kincaid, Jonathan Clements, Loretta Holmes, Paulo Coelho, Michelle Berger, Jane Dentinger, Cindy Karamitis, Catherine Wallach, Steve Irby, David Mills, Tina-marie Duff, Richard and Joy Newcombe, John Taylor, Kelsey Amble, Brian and Lisa McCarthy, Laurie Balut, Jeannine and Brad Dillon, Sam Honen, John Webster, Sabila Khan, Joan Louise Brookbank, Susan Stalzer, Roger Cooper, Toula Polygalaktos, Cathy McCarthy, Elizabeth Lazenby, Robin Posner, Sandy Strk, Jennifer Walsh, Ray Casazza, Anne-Marie and Anthony Rutella, Beth Goehring, Sharon Fantera, Larry Shapiro, Laura Balducci, Cynthia Clarke, Doreen Sinski, John "The Sarge" Miller, Raquel Avila, John and Winifred Jansen, Liz Kirmss, Jean Bjork, Steve Scarallo, Anthony Cole, Jill Fabiani, Noelle Kuchler, Patricia Clement, Pam Fitzgerald, Ellen Giesow, Karen Strejlau, Amalia Buendia, Michael and Fran Bartholomew, Nancy Schleyer, Sal Grasso, Jr., Maria Theresa Gutierrez, Janet Shavel, Kathy Vella, Robert and Maureen Sullivan, Marc Vital-

Herne, Estelle Peck, Patricia Schreck, Maddalena Pennino, Jennifer Kanakos, Audrey Puzzo, Deborah Sinclaire, Jay Franco, Lisa Thornbloom, Jessica Walles, Kalyani Fernando, Eric Zagrans, Patrick Coleman, Clark Strand, Mitch Horowitz, Michael Manning, Maria Tahim, Kathy Viele, Alexander Shaia, Kathy Powell, and Jessica Rey.

To Father Andrzej Zglejszewski, you changed my life. Without you this book would not exist. Thank you for lighting a flame inside me.

To George Weigel, thank you for stretching my mind and for your wicked sense of humor. It has been a pleasure swapping stories about history, baseball, theology, and bourbon.

To Will "Sticks" Romano, a phenomenal friend, musician and writer, thank you for always being there and laying down the rhythm.

To James Philipps, thank you for being one of my greatest teachers and for your enduring friendship.

To Bert, Frances, Josephine, Lenny, and Carrie Poppi, thank you for your love and patience over the years.

To all the folks at Panera in Rockville Centre, New York, especially Christian Alexandre, thank you for your kindness and for always remembering my name. I wrote three books there, sitting by a window and drinking coffee. It feels a little like a home away from home except that it's usually crowded with people I don't know.

To Maura Zagrans, your love and support and energy have been infectious and I am eternally grateful for all the small and big things you do. These are just signposts of the enormity of your heart. Oh, and you make Jack Kerouac proud.

To Dr. Issam and Kathy Nemeh, thank you for your faith and passion.

To Mary Ann and Ted Winkowski, thank you for your support and kindheartedness and the laughs and love. I feel so blessed to know you and delight in your friendship. Mary Ann, it is your unique vision that has changed the way I will look at everything forever.

To Annie Leuenberger, you are one of the greats. Thank you.

To Justin Fatica, love your energy, brother! Thank you for all your strength and for motivating me to take chances.

To Jennifer Puglisi, always good to have you on my side. Thank you for always being there.

To Audrey and Alex Robles, Johnny and Elvira Diaz, the Diaz Family, and all the Water Walkers, thank you for the strength of your faith and for teaching me to get out of the boat and walk, walk, walk.

To Michael "Leo" McCormack, thank you for being one of my greatest friends and thank you for lighting a fire under my butt to "do something." Thanks for all the laughs and beers.

To Courtney Snyder, whether you know it or not, you inspire me and I thank you for your friendship.

To my mom, Roseanne Jansen, my sisters, Annie, Mary, Suzie, and Julie, and my grandparents Nan and Harry, thank you for your love and for everything over the years. You have blessed me in so many ways.

To my dad, wherever you are, you are missed.

To my BFF, you know who you are and you know what I want to say.

Lastly, to Grace, Eddie, and Charlie, you are the loves of my life. Thank you for rearranging the stars for me.

Peace.

GARY JANSEN, author of *The Rosary: A Journey to the Beloved,* is an editor at Doubleday Religion and the former editor-in-chief of the Quality Paperback Book Club. His writing has appeared in *USA Today, Newsday,* and the *Chicago Sun Times.*